Houghton
Mifflin
Harcourt

JOURNEYS

Close Reader

GRADE

6

Consumable

UNIT 1
Cultural Connections

UNIT 2
Finding Your Voice

UNIT 3
Exploring the Limits

UNIT 4
Tales from the Past

UNIT 5
Taking Risks

UNIT 6
Reading Adventures

Houghton
Mifflin
Harcourt

Journeys
Close Reader

UNIT 1
Cultural Connections

Background What would your self-portrait look like? Many of Mexican painter Frida Kahlo's self-portraits revealed her physical pain or her love for her country. In this text, you'll read about Kahlo's life and how her art changed as she grew older.

Setting a Purpose Read the text to learn about the life and work of Frida Kahlo.

Frida Kahlo: Portrait of an Artist

Narrative Nonfiction by Fiona O'Connor

CLOSE READ
Notes

(1) Read As you read, collect and cite text evidence.

- Circle details that tell about Frida's personality.
- Underline text that explains what caused Frida to begin painting.

Early Life

Frida Kahlo (1907–1954) planned to be a doctor, but a bus accident when she was in her late teens led her to become an artist instead. Frida was born in Mexico City in 1907. As a child, she was
5 **stricken** with polio, a virus that kills nerve cells in the spine. She was not **paralyzed** like many other polio victims. As a result of her illness, however, one of her legs became very weak. To

stricken: effected by a diseage

paralyzed: cant move a part of a body.

2

strengthen her leg muscles, her father suggested that she
10 play soccer, wrestle, and swim. Frida did all three, even
though most girls at the time would not have dreamed of
participating in **unladylike** activities such as sports!

   In 1922, Frida entered the National Preparatory School
in Mexico City as one of only thirty-five girls in the school.
15 From the start, Frida stood out. She was friendly and
popular. She liked to wear bright Mexican-style clothing
and chunky jewelry. Her long skirts hid the fact that one of
her legs remained thinner than the other. Even though she
studied medicine, she was very interested in art. When the
20 famous artist Diego Rivera painted murals in the school
auditorium, Frida spent hours studying his work.

A Life-Changing Event

One fateful day in 1925, Frida was traveling on a public bus
when it **collided** with a streetcar. Frida's hips and spine were
badly injured, forcing her to undergo multiple operations
25 and stay in the hospital for many weeks. Then she had to
spend months in bed at home. Used to being active, Frida
became very bored. To keep herself busy while she was
bedridden, she took up painting. She hoped that she could
sell some of her paintings to support her family.

unladylike:

not polite
or quiet in
a way that
was thought
for a proper
lady

collided:

crash into

bedridden:

forced to
stay in bed

---

2 **Reread** Reread lines 13–29. What events in Frida Kahlo's life led her to begin painting? Cite details from the text in your answer.

In 1922, Frida entered the National Preporation School. She became very intrested in art. In 1925 she colid into a street car. Fridas hips and spin were badly injured. While she was bedridden she got intrested in art.

3

③ Read As you read, collect and cite text evidence.

- Underline details that describe Frida's paintings.
- Circle text that explains the meaning behind each painting.
- Draw a box around text that tells how Frida influenced other artists.

A New Direction

30 Frida's first work was of herself, entitled *Self-Portrait Wearing a Velvet Dress.* The style of this painting is formal. She portrays herself wearing an **elegant** red velvet gown against a dark background. Her serious expression matches the mood of the painting. As she

35 continued painting self-portraits over the years, her style **evolved.** She began to use her paintings to express her feelings of pride in Mexico. She portrayed herself wearing her colorful traditional Mexican clothing. She included symbols of the Aztec culture, such as the

40 hummingbird. Exotic flowers and wildlife found in Mexico filled the backgrounds of many of her paintings.

elegant:

evolved:

An Autobiographical Painter

Frida is sometimes called an "autobiographical painter." Through her art, she depicts important events in her life and shares her feelings about her experiences. For

45 example, the painting *The Two Fridas* shows two images of herself, one in traditional Mexican dress and the other in modern clothing. Their hearts are exposed, and the Mexican Frida's heart is leaking blood. This painting expresses her heartbreak over the conflict in her

50 marriage to Diego Rivera, the muralist she first met at her school. In a portrait in 1938, a broken stone column replaces her spine, symbolizing the condition of her back

and the constant pain she suffered as a result of the bus
accident thirteen years before. A self-portrait in 1951, one of

55 her final works, portrays Frida in a wheelchair. She could
no longer walk.

Frida's Legacy

Frida died in 1954 at the age of 47. During her lifetime,
many people thought her paintings were "weird." She didn't
make herself look pretty in her self-portraits. She painted

60 herself as she was and as she felt at the time. She once said
that her paintings were "the **frankest** expression of herself."
Other artists were influenced by her honesty. They realized
that it was acceptable to paint what they felt and thought.
Today, Frida Kahlo is considered to be an important artist

65 in Mexico and internationally.

frankest:

④ Reread and Discuss Reread lines 30–56. Discuss how Frida Kahlo's life and
art changed as she grew older. Cite evidence from the text in your discussion.

SHORT RESPONSE

Cite Text Evidence How was Frida's accident reflected in her art? Cite text evidence
in your response.

Her accident reflected in
her art by making
here art be sad lik for
expample she painted a picture
of here in a wheel char
because wold never walk
again.

5

Background Poetry comes in many forms, from longer narrative poems that tell a story to short haiku that describe a single moment. In this text, you'll read three poems about sports. Two are limericks—funny rhyming poems with a familiar pattern of three long and two short lines—and one is a narrative poem.

Setting a Purpose Read the sports poems to learn how each speaker feels about his or her sport.

Sporty Poetry

Poetry

CLOSE READ
Notes

① **Read** As you read, collect and cite text evidence.
- Underline text that describes the speaker in each limerick.
- Circle the unexpected twist or punch line in each poem.

A poem about sports, like Jerry Spinelli's "Goal to Go," can capture the tumult of an exciting game or a pursuit downfield. It can capture a miraculous victory or a contested call by an
5   umpire who said a base-stealer was safe when the culprit seemed to be out! A sports poem can reveal the **agony** of split-second decision making on the field, as "To Steal or Not to Steal?" does. Sports poems can also be funny, like the two
10   limericks on the next page.

agony:

torture

Two Limericks

by Rob Hale

When I step on the basketball court,
They all **jeer,** "In your dreams! You're too short!"
Do I get in a **funk**?
Nope. (I calmly slam dunk.)
5   I would say I'm a pretty good sport.

A bicycle racer named Raleigh
Told the cheering crowd, "Thanks! But, by golly,
I couldn't have done it—
I'd never have won it—
5   (Without my dear passenger, Wally!")

jeer:
make rude insults

funk:
to get in a bad mood.

② Reread   Reread both limericks. Describe the speaker in each poem. Cite text evidence in your answer.

Short, basketball player, bicycle racer, kind. I step on the basketball court, In your dreams! Your too short. Without my dear friend wally, A bicycle racer named Raleigh.

③ **Read** As you read, collect and cite text evidence.

- Circle text that tells where the speaker is at the beginning of the poem and what the speaker decides to do.
- Underline how the speaker feels about that decision.

To Steal or Not to Steal?

Safely here at second base,
I try to read my coach's face.
He's stroking his chin,
On his lips a slight grin.

5 Is that a signal for me to steal?
Or is he thinking of his next meal?
Sighing, I study the pitcher next.
His actions leave me as **perplexed.**
He winds up, then **abruptly** stops.

10 Into his glove—up, down—the ball plops.
Summoning my courage, to myself I say,
"Stealing and scoring could save the day."

perplexed:
confused

abruptly:
suddenly

summoning:
calling

So off I sprint, almost there
Before the pitcher is even aware.
15   Whack! The ball is hit at last,
I round third, racing fast.
My cleats are digging in the dirt,
The wind is tugging at my shirt.
Heading home at **breakneck** speed,
20   Another moment is all I need.
With a mighty grunt, **hurtling** through the air,
I slide into the plate, and *Safe!* they declare!
Though in the end we lose the game
And will not earn our championship fame,
25   I think about what I have done;
In my heart, I know I've won.
I made a decision. I did my best.
I gave all for my team. I passed the test.

breakneck:
very fast

hurtling:
flying

---

④ Reread and Discuss   Reread "To Steal or Not to Steal?" Discuss the theme of the poem. What message is the poet sending? Cite evidence from the text in your discussion.

SHORT RESPONSE

Cite Text Evidence   How does the speaker in this poem compare to the speaker in the first limerick? Do they share any traits? Cite text evidence in your response.

That it doesn't matter [other evidence: In my heart I know I've won. I made a decision, I did my best.]
how you did or how you look
you can do you best and people
might be mean but dont listen
and know that you are amazing
and you did good. And the evidence.
"They all jeering your dreams your
to short. do I get in a funk nope. I calmly slam dunk.

9

Background Did you ever wonder how people wrote things down before paper was invented? Or how people learned about the world before there were books? In this text, you'll read about the inventions that led to the kinds of books we know today.

Setting a Purpose Read the text to learn about the history of the book.

History of the Book

Informational Text

CLOSE READ
Notes

1 Read As you read, collect and cite text evidence.

- Circle each of the materials and tools people have used to record information.
- Underline text that describes big changes in the way information was recorded.

vibrant:

A full of energy and enthusiasum.

Throughout history, people have found ways to present their ideas. Writers have been recording their thoughts for thousands of years. These expressions from the past are not muted, but
5 remain **vibrant** and meaningful.

Books have an important place in the timeline of recorded thought. This timeline runs from ancient symbols recorded on paper to the electronic books of our own time.

10 People are always looking for better ways to record
information and ideas. The ancient Egyptians used a form
of paper called papyrus. Papyrus was made from a plant
that grew along the Nile River.

The ancient Babylonians used clay tablets to record
15 everything from goat sales to literary works. They even
used clay tablets to record the first known map of the world.
With this system, though, it was not easy to make **revisions**
to a manuscript.

Parchment was a material made from the skin of sheep
20 or goats. It was developed during the Roman Empire.
Parchment lasted longer than papyrus.

Until the late 700s C.E., text had to be written and
copied by hand. Book printing began in China around 868,
but the type could be used only once. Around 1050, a
25 Chinese printer named Bi Sheng invented movable type.
Movable type could be used over and over.

Perhaps the biggest printing breakthrough came in
Germany in the 1440s when Johannes Gutenberg developed
a printing press. Movable type was set in a wooden form.
30 The letters were coated with ink. Then a sheet of paper was
laid on the letters and pressed with a wooden plate, creating
an entire printed page.

revisions:

a
action
of revising

2 Reread Reread lines 10–32. Why was the invention of book printing
important? How did movable type and the printing press improve the process?

Movable type could be
used over and over. The printing
press was the big breakthrough.

(3) Read As you read, collect and cite text evidence.

- In the timeline, circle inventions since Gutenberg's press.
- In the text, circle each new invention in publishing.
- Underline the results of each new invention.

Milestones in the History of the Book

3200 B.C.E. Egyptian papyrus scrolls

3000 B.C.E.

2300 B.C.E. Babylonian clay tablets

2000 B.C.E.

1000 B.C.E.

190 B.C.E. Parchment codex

100 B.C.E.

500 C.E.

868 C.E. Early printed book
1050 Movable type
1440–1450 The Gutenberg press

1500 C.E.

1600 C.E.

1800 C.E.

1884 The Linotype machine
1931 Audio books

2000 C.E. **2000** eBooks

From Linotype to Online Type

In the 1880s, the publishing **industry** once again changed
drastically. A man named Ottmar Mergenthaler invented
35 the Linotype machine, which allowed its operator to use a
keyboard to type the text. The Linotype machine created
molds from lines of type (the process for which the machine
was named). Text became cheaper to produce. The public
began pressuring the industry to print more. People wanted
40 both the wry humor of Mark Twain and the serious news of
the day.

    The first audio books were developed in 1931 by the
American Foundation for the Blind. These books were
known as "talking books." In the 1960s, talking books
45 became popular with the public.

    Today, the newest and fastest way to publish a book is
electronically. An author can publish his or her own work
on the Internet or as an eBook. The electronic process saves
paper. However, an eBook may still go through several steps
50 before publication. Many eBooks are available for free in
electronic form on several websites, including one named
Project Gutenberg in honor of one of the giants in the
history of the book.

industry:

drastically:

④ Reread and Discuss Reread lines 33–53. Discuss how modern inventions
have made books cheaper and easier to get. Cite text evidence in your discussion.

SHORT RESPONSE

Cite Text Evidence Based on the timeline, which time period saw the most
inventions? How does the text support this observation?

1800 to 2000 because
there were the most inventions
in that time.

Background Imagine seeing two elephants on opposite sides of a concrete wall and physically sensing—but not hearing—that they are communicating. That's what happened to Katy Payne at the Portland Zoo in 1984. Four months later, she used listening equipment to prove she was right. This text provides details of her discovery.

Setting a Purpose Read the text and view the graphics to learn why people can't hear the communications of elephants and many other creatures.

Silent Noise

Informational Text by Jacqueline Adams

CLOSE READ
Notes

① Read As you read, collect and cite text evidence.

- Underline clues that led Payne to think elephants were communicating even when they seemed to be silent.
- Circle the mystery Payne's discovery helped solve.

prick:

a puncture made by needle, thorn, or the like.

Dog owners are accustomed to seeing their pets **prick** their ears when everything seems silent. Like many animals, dogs hear sounds that are beyond human reach.

5   Biologist Katy Payne listened to elephants communicate at a zoo in Portland, Oregon. Even when the elephants seemed to be silent, she felt the air throb. It reminded her of the throbbing from a pipe organ's low, doleful tones.

10   Payne began to wonder if elephants made noises not heard by humans. She recorded the elephants with devices that pick up sounds below the range of human hearing. She discovered a torrent of rumbling. "There was a whole communication system down there that people hadn't

15 known about," she said. This would help solve an elephant mystery that had puzzled biologists for years.

How Low Can You Go?

Biologists have heard a wide range of elephant sounds, from mothers' gentle rumblings as they coaxed their calves along to urgent trumpeting that warned of danger. But how

20 elephants kept track of each other in the wild remained a mystery. Elephants lived clustered in groups that stayed a couple of miles apart but traveled in the same direction. When one group changed direction, other groups swiveled to follow. How did the elephants know what faraway groups

25 were doing?

    The mystery was solved when Payne discovered that elephants communicate with **infrasonic** sound. Because low-pitched transmissions travel farther, elephants can communicate over long distances.

infrasonic:

nothing or pertaining to a sound wave with a frequency below the audio frequency range.

② Reread Reread lines 10–29. Summarize what Payne discovered and the mystery her discovery helped solve.

She discoverd elephants communicate using sounds below = like low organ's low, doteful tones. The mystery was solved when Payne discoverd the elephants communacate

③ **Read** As you read, collect and cite text evidence.

- Underline the process explained in the text that the diagram helps you visualize.
- On the diagram, label the outer ear.
- Circle text that explains how bats use their hearing.

Catch the Wave

30 Sound energy travels in waves. When sound waves reach the outer ear, they are **funneled** inside, starting a chain reaction. The eardrum vibrates, moving tiny bones in the middle ear and passing the waves to the inner ear.

The number of waves that travel each second is a
35 sound's frequency, measured in hertz (Hz). The human ear is tuned to hear frequencies between 20 and 20,000 Hz. You can compare this range to the ranges heard by other animals by examining the chart on the next page.

funneled: flue, tube, or shaft as a ventilation

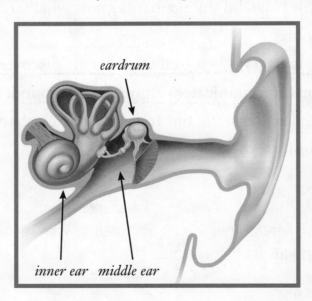

eardrum

inner ear   middle ear

Squeaks and Chirps

Animals such as dogs, dolphins, and bats go to the
40 opposite extreme from elephants. They pick up supersonic, or **ultrasonic,** sound frequencies. These sounds are above the range of human hearing.

ultrasonic: of, relating, or utilizing ultrasound

Even though bats can see, sight isn't enough for finding insects at night. Bats send out a clamor of supersonic chirps

45 into what looks like a dark void. These high-frequency waves bounce off insects and come back to tell the bat where the insects are. To humans, what seems like a quiet night is filled with "silent" noise!

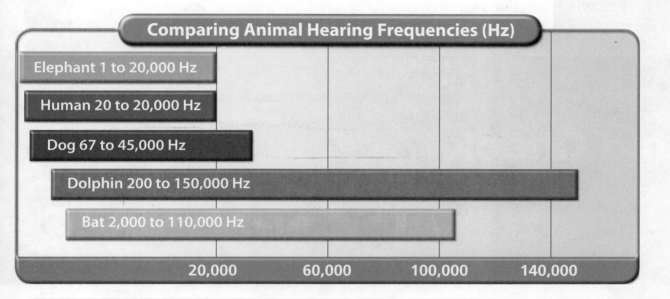

Comparing Animal Hearing Frequencies (Hz)

Elephant 1 to 20,000 Hz

Human 20 to 20,000 Hz

Dog 67 to 45,000 Hz

Dolphin 200 to 150,000 Hz

Bat 2,000 to 110,000 Hz

20,000   60,000   100,000   140,000

④ Reread and Discuss Reread lines 30–48. Discuss what supersonic sound frequencies are and how bats use them. Then discuss whether you would like to have supersonic hearing and give at least one reason.

SHORT RESPONSE

Cite Text Evidence   How does the bar graph support information in the text? What does the graph tell you that the text does not? Cite details from both in your response.

It shows how far bats can communacatio with Hz.

Background Family singing groups, like the Trapp Family Singers, the Jackson Five, and the Jonas Brothers, have been around for a long time. It makes sense: families spend a lot of time together. Singing is fun and it's something almost everyone can do. In this text, a singing family prepares for a show.

Setting a Purpose Read the play to learn about the importance of following directions carefully.

Sound Check

Readers' Theater by Joel Mallery

CLOSE READ
Notes

① Read As you read, collect and cite text evidence.

- Underline the steps for setting up the sound system.
- Circle dialogue that reveals what Elisa is worrying about.

Cast of Characters

Elisa Santos, age 12

Manny Santos, age 15

Anna Santos, age 10

Elena Santos (Mom)

Pedro Santos (Dad)

Setting: Elisa's middle school, Portland, Oregon.

Elisa: Hurry up, Manny! We still have tons to do.

Manny: Elisa, relax. You have this annoying tendency to get worked up before a show. I don't need the tension.

5 **Elisa:** Aren't you **concerned** about my welfare? We're singing in front of my school and my friends.

Manny: You should give your family a little more credit. We're **professionals.** Dad knows every aspect of the music business.

10 **Elisa:** I know, but what if I hit a wrong note?

Anna: La-la-la-la-la . . . What? I'm just doing my scales.

Manny: I think we should all focus predominantly on setting up the sound system. Read me the directions, Elisa.

Elisa: Okay. I'm sure I did the first one.

15 1. Plug in the **amplifier.**

2. Put the instruments and the microphones where they belong on the stage.

Anna: I'm on it!

concerned:

trouded or anxioux.

professionals:

appropriate to a profesion

amplifier:

an electronic mponent or circet for amptfying power.

---

② **Reread** Reread lines 2–18. In your own words, describe the first two steps of setting up a sound system. What does Elisa say she's already done?

1. Plug the cord into the amplifier
2. Prt the musical suplics back where they belong. Elisa said "Okay, Im pretty sure
3. I did the firstone."

3 Read As you read, collect and cite text evidence.

- Underline the remaining steps in setting up the sound system.
- Circle the problem and its solution.

Elisa: Shh! Where was I?

20   3. Connect the correct cords to the guitar, keyboard, and microphones.

    4. Plug all cords into the amplifier.

    5. Connect the speaker cords to the amplifier and then to the speakers.

25 **Manny:** Nothing is happening. Hmm, I think we may genuinely have a problem.

Mom: Is everything ready for the **performance**?

Elisa: Mom, Dad, thank goodness you're here. We don't have any sound!

30 **Dad:** Really? I can hear you just fine.

Elisa: Dad! This is my worst nightmare and you're making jokes!

Mom: Did you check that the correct cords are connected?

35 **Manny:** Yes. See where they're running parallel to the stage?

Mom: The speakers are plugged in to the amplifier.

Anna: Hey, did we try this plug?

Manny: Wow! Plugging in the amp! What an

40 innovation!

Elisa: I guess I forgot to do Step 1.

performance:

20

© Houghton Mifflin Harcourt Publishing Company

CLOSE READ
Notes

Dad: That's okay. Luckily, Anna was here.

Anna: I guess I supply the power in this family.

Mom: Aptly put, Anna!

45 **Dad:** Great idea for a new song! Here's to Anna, the hero of the hour! Just plug her in and she'll supply the power!

④ Reread and Discuss Reread the play. Discuss which character takes everything the most seriously and why that might be. Cite evidence from the text in your discussion.

SHORT RESPONSE

Cite Text Evidence What is the moment of greatest tension in the play, and how is it resolved? What lesson can readers infer from these events? Support your response with details from the text.

The moment with the most tension
is when the amplifier wasnt working.
"They had no sound." It was resolved
because Anna plugged in the cord.

21

UNIT 2
Finding Your Voice

Background An argument can take many forms, from a passionate disagreement between friends to a calm, well-reasoned opinion essay. Advertisements and letters to the editor are also arguments. They try to convince readers to think or act a certain way. The key for readers is to evaluate whether their claims are valid and fact-based.

Setting a Purpose Read the text to learn more about advertisements and letters to the editor and how to think independently about them.

Persuading the Public

Informational Text by Cecelia Munzenmaier

CLOSE READ
Notes

(1) **Read** As you read, collect and cite text evidence.

- Underline how many advertisements most Americans see daily.
- Circle the goals of advertising and persuasive writing.

advertisements:

Most Americans see or hear more than two hundred **advertisements** each day. They read them in magazines, newspapers, mail, and e-mail. They hear them on the radio. They see

5 them on television, on billboards, and in skywriting.

The goal of **commercial** advertising is to persuade people to buy things. Other forms of persuasion try to influence how people think. **Editorials** or letters to the editor, for example, express an opinion. They present an argument and give reasons why people should agree with that particular point of view.

Ads Attract Attention!

Advertisements use pictures, **slogans,** and **celebrities** to get people's attention. Ads often include a call to action. That message tells people how to improve their lives, usually by buying a certain product. Public service advertising campaigns also seek to persuade people. They do not promote a product. Instead, they give people information about how to make better choices. A public service announcement (PSA) might urge people to exercise, be tolerant of others, or recycle.

commercial:

editorials:

slogans:

celebrities:

②**Reread** Reread lines 1–21. How are commercial advertisements and public service campaigns different?

_____

_____

_____

_____

③ **Read** As you read, collect and cite text evidence.

- Draw a check mark next to the benefit of subscribing to *Persuade* magazine.
- Underline words in the soup ad meant to convince you to buy the soup.
- Circle all the slogans you find in the ads.

subscribe:

This online ad is aimed at selling magazines. It offers a discount to attract consumers.

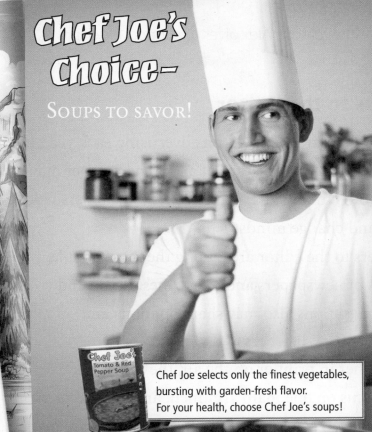

This commercial ad (left) uses marketing flair—a slogan and a company celebrity—to promote a brand of soup. This public-service ad (right) uses a catchy slogan and effective pictures to persuade people not to litter.

Chef Joe selects only the finest vegetables, bursting with garden-fresh flavor. For your health, choose Chef Joe's soups!

④ **Reread** Reread the ad copy for Chef Joe's soups. What two claims does the ad make about the soups? What evidence is provided to support the claims?

_____

_____

_____

_____

⑤ Read As you read, collect and cite text evidence.

- Underline a reason for writing a letter to the editor and details about what makes an effective letter.
- Circle the claim made by Alex Sims in his letter to the editor.
- Underline the reasons Alex gives to support his claim.

Letters to the Editor

Billions of dollars are spent on advertising each year, but mailing a letter to the editor of a local newspaper may be just as powerful. It can be an effective way to persuade
25 people and change minds.

Letters to the editor are among the most popular **features** of newspapers and magazines. Radio and television stations also may share opinions and comments from listeners and viewers.

30 Whether in print or on the air, the most effective letters focus on one main argument and present facts and reasons to support it. Readers or listeners are invited to consider, and perhaps share, a point of view. The letter on the next page provides a good example.

features:

35 To the Editor of the Sentinel:

I believe our new gym should be named for Coach Len Burns.

Coach made all kids feel a part of the team, whether they were stars or reserve players. He taught us not to gloat
40 when we won. He taught us not to give up when we lost. He gave us the confidence to face any showdown.

For thirty years, he has been a phenomenal coach. His lessons have lingered for many athletes. That's why the new gymnasium should be named for Len Burns. He is the man
45 who taught us how to be good players and good sports.

Sincerely,
Alex Sims, basketball player
Hoyt Middle School

6 Reread and Discuss Reread lines 35–45. Discuss whether Alex Sims makes a good argument and why. Support your opinion with details from the letter.

SHORT RESPONSE

Cite Text Evidence   Review the ads and the letter to the editor. Which is the most persuasive? Which is the least persuasive? Support your opinions with text evidence.

_____

_____

_____

_____

_____

Background How would you like to learn to do a trick with knots that will dazzle your friends and family? This text provides you with step-by-step instructions for how to do that. It also provides clear illustrations to help you visualize each step.

Setting a Purpose Read the text and use the diagrams to learn how to perform a knot trick.

The Knot That Is Not

Informational Text illustrated by Michael Garland

CLOSE READ
Notes

1 Read As you read, collect and cite text evidence.

- Underline each action the text directs you to take.
- Circle what the text tells you to say to your audience.

STEP 1

loose single knot

Take one thick shoelace and tie a loose knot in the center. Keep that knot loose so your audience can see a little daylight through it. Hold the shoelace up to your audience and say: "See that I have made a knot in this
5   shoelace!"

STEP 2

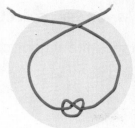

Let the audience examine it. Then take the two ends of
the shoelace and cross them, a few inches from the top.
Tell the audience: "I will now trap this bottom knot in its
place with a series of tight, locking knots at the top."

STEP 3

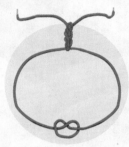

10   Tie the crossed ends into a knot, leaving some extra
shoelace to work with. Then tie a second knot on top of
the first. Then tie a third knot on top of that. You should
now have three tight "locking" knots at the top and still
one loose knot at the bottom.

STEP 4

15   Announce: "I will now try to untie the bottom knot
while keeping all the other knots locked **securely** in
place." Add: "Even though that seems physically
impossible to do!"

securely:

---

(2) **Reread**   Reread Steps 1–4. What change do you make in the shoelace in Step 2?
What does the diagram in Step 3 help you understand?

_____

_____

_____

③ **Read** As you read, collect and cite text evidence.
- Circle each separate action you take in Step 5.
- Underline and number each action you take in Step 6.

STEP 5

Now place the knotted shoelace behind your back where
20 the audience cannot see it. Struggle mightily with your
hands, arms, and torso.

STEP 6

Pretend you are trying to untie the knot while you are
really doing the following:
- Feel for the loose knot.
25 - Open it up.
- Spread the knot out with both hands until it rises to
the top and joins the other three knots.

With a great **flourish,** return the shoelace to the front
where the audience can see it. Hold it up and announce:

30 "The bottom knot, as you can
see, has now disappeared!"

Take a bow.

Only you know
that the bottom
35 knot has not
disappeared.
You simply moved
it to the top!

flourish:

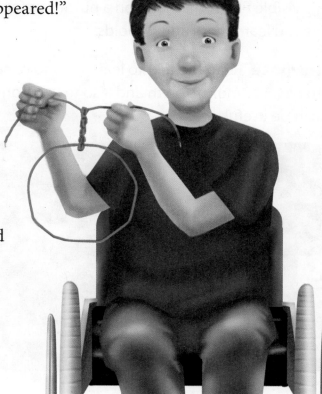

④ **Reread and Discuss** Reread lines 19–32. Discuss whether Steps 5 and 6 should
be combined, split up differently, or left as they are. Provide reasons for your opinion.

SHORT RESPONSE

Cite Text Evidence What is the key to dazzling an audience with this trick? What parts of
Steps 4, 5, and 6 help you accomplish this? Cite text evidence in your response.

_____

_____

_____

_____

_____

_____

Background Did you know that millions of mold spores are floating in the air all around you right now? They are too small to see with just your eyes, but these single-celled reproductive units will quickly multiply into a visible fuzz if they land on a nutritious food source. This text helps you learn more about molds.

Setting a Purpose Read the text to learn how to conduct an experiment to observe mold growth and also to learn one way in which mold can be useful.

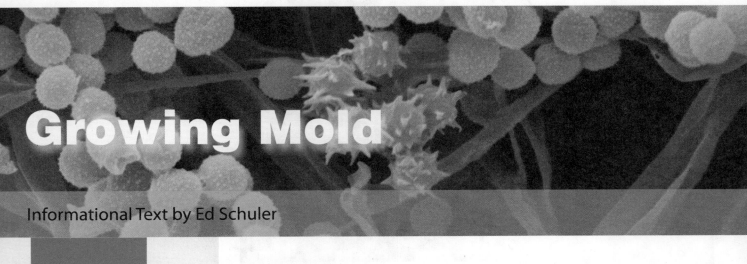

Growing Mold

Informational Text by Ed Schuler

CLOSE READ
Notes

(1) **Read** As you read, collect and cite text evidence.
- Underline the sentence that tells what mold is.
- Circle the subheadings and other text features in the experiment that help make it clear.

microscopic:

organic:

You're hungry. You grab some bread. Ewwww! It's moldy. This may be a question you're reluctant to ask, but what is mold, anyway?

Mold is a type of fungus, a **microscopic**
5 organism that grows on **organic** matter such as food. Mold eats bacteria, which, as you'll read, can sometimes be a good thing!

As a detached observer, you can see for yourself how mold grows under different conditions. You might even learn a scientific principle or two while you're at it!

A Moldy Experiment

What You Need

- bread (three dry slices)
- cheese (three medium-hard slices)
- tomato (three slices)
- plastic wrap
- plastic knife
- small paper plates

What To Do

1. Make three separate groups, each with a slice of bread, cheese, and tomato. Cut each slice in half. If using three foods is too complex, you can compromise and use one.
2. In Group A, wrap a half-slice of each food in plastic. Leave the rest unwrapped.
3. In Group B, put one set of halves in a dark cupboard. Put the others in an indoor location that has **constant** light.

constant:

4. In Group C, put one set in a warm, dark place. Put the others in a refrigerator.
5. Check your samples **daily** for a week. Notice how mold forms as food changes (becomes shriveled or fuzzy) through decomposition.

daily:

2 Reread Reread lines 11–25. If you follow the steps without compromising, what will each group consist of? What do you suppose each group is meant to test?

_____

_____

_____

_____

_____

③ Read As you read, collect and cite text evidence.

- Circle the two questions that would help you determine which foods molds grow best on.
- Underline the question that would help you figure out whether mold grows better when exposed to air.
- Circle the name of a medicine made from mold.

STEP 2

STEP 3

STEP 4

What To Look For

- Which foods grow mold first? Which foods grow the most mold?
- Which food has more mold on it, the wrapped food or the unwrapped food?

30
- What relationships do you see between mold growth and location? Does mold grow better in light or darkness? in warm or cool places?

Fleming's Miracle Mold

Mold once helped scientists find an elegant solution to a big problem.

35   In 1928 a Scottish scientist named Alexander Fleming was working in a hospital lab, hoping to find a way to fight **bacterial** infection. To study bacteria, Fleming grew specimens in dishes. One day, he noticed that a mold had grown on one specimen. Then he discovered
40   that around the mold, bacteria had died.

      What had killed them? It was a chemical in the mold!

bacterial:

After years of further research, scientists used the mold, *Penicillium notatum,* to make a drug called penicillin. At first, penicillin was hard to make in large batches. Then
45 scientists found that it grew fast on corn and rotting melon.

    By the mid-1940s, the United States was making 650 billion **doses** of penicillin per month. Infections that once were deadly could now be cured with an antibiotic drug made from a mold!

doses:

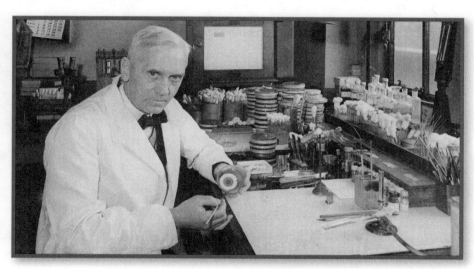

Alexander Fleming in his lab in 1952

④ Reread and Discuss   Reread lines 33–49. Discuss what Alexander Fleming discovered and why it was "an elegant solution to a big problem." Cite text details in your discussion.

SHORT RESPONSE

Cite Text Evidence Was penicillin a popular drug in the 1940s? Why or why not? Cite text evidence to support your response.

_____

_____

_____

_____

_____

Background There are too many islands on our globe to count. Nevertheless, scientists have been able to figure out how most of these islands were formed. Some broke off of continents. Others "grew" from layers of lava or from a buildup of coral. Some were even made by people! This text explains two ways islands are formed.

Setting a Purpose Read the text to learn about different kinds of island and how each is formed.

Exploring Islands

Informational Text by Carole Gerber

CLOSE READ
Notes

① **Read** As you read, collect and cite text evidence.

- Underline the definition of an island.
- Circle the two main types of island as well as the specific kind of island that is found along the Atlantic Coast of North America.

Picture an island. What comes to mind? Maybe it's a sparsely inhabited Pacific island with immaculately white sand, where only a few seabirds venture. Maybe it's Greenland, the
5   world's biggest island, at 822,000 square miles. It could be the island nation of Indonesia, home to 211 million people.

Islands come in all **varieties.** They defy one-size-fits-all descriptions—except for the rudimentary one that applies

10 to all islands: a piece of land completely surrounded by water.

How Islands Form

There are two main types of island—oceanic and continental. Both types show the consequences of dramatic changes.

15   Oceanic islands, such as those found along the coast of Southern California, form from the peaks of undersea volcanoes. Some oceanic islands are created when coral reefs, made from rigid coral skeletons, build up around these volcanoes.

20   Continental islands form when the sea rises and surrounds a section of the mainland of a continent. One kind of continental island is the barrier island. This island forms from the action of water, wind, and tides that shape and move sand and **sediment.** Many barrier islands are

25 found along the Atlantic coast of North America.

varieties:

sediment:

(2) **Reread** Reread lines 12–25. Which type of island is a barrier island—oceanic or continental? Explain why, citing details from the text.

_____

_____

_____

_____

_____

③ **Read** As you read, collect and cite text evidence.

- In the diagram, underline the five different zones of a barrier island.
- Circle text that explains what the diagram shows.
- In the margin, write another term from the text that means the same as "overwash area."

Barrier Island Zones

Barrier islands are always poised for change. A typical barrier island has five zones. Ocean waves bring sand to the beach. Wind forms the sand into dunes that are held in place by plants. Storms push water permeated with
30 sediment over the dunes, forming a mud flat. Ocean tides make an area of salt **marsh** around the mud flats.

marsh:

Five Zones of a Barrier Island

1. sea
2. beach
3. dune area
4. overwash area
5. marsh

The Island Ecosystem

The Outer Banks are a chain of barrier islands along the North Carolina coast. This island **ecosystem** is the home of a rich array of plant and sea life.
35 Some animals live on the Outer Banks year-round, but others only visit. Often, the sky above the islands is filled with flocks of snow geese and other birds that

ecosystem:

arrive for the winter. Another visitor, the female loggerhead sea turtle, lives in the ocean but comes ashore in summer to
40 dig a nest and lay her eggs.

To care for this ecosystem and protect its animals and plants, portions of the Outer Banks have been named federal wildlife refuges.

Female loggerhead sea turtles return to the Outer Banks every two to three years to nest.

④ Reread and Discuss Reread lines 26–31. Discuss what you have learned about barrier island zones, citing details from both the text and the diagram.

SHORT RESPONSE

Cite Text Evidence What does the information provided earlier in this selection help you understand about the Outer Banks? Use text evidence to support your response.

_____

_____

_____

_____

_____

Background Traditions exist in all cultures. There are traditions for celebrating and mourning, and traditions that remind a people of who they are and of their place in the world. You may be familiar with the traditional arts of Native Americans, or perhaps you've been to a powwow. Native American traditions extend into poetry as well.

Setting a Purpose Read the text to see how the traditions of three Native American cultures are expressed in poetry.

Native American Poetry

Poetry

CLOSE READ
Notes

① **Read** As you read, collect and cite text evidence.

- Circle where each Native American culture is located.
- In "Twelfth Song of Thunder," underline words and phrases that describe the voice and where it is heard.

tradition:

The Native American poems in this selection connect to a rich cultural past. The Makah Nation of Washington State retains tribal dancing as an important part of its heritage.
5   "Song" honors that **tradition.** "Twelfth Song of Thunder" celebrates the Navajo of the American Southwest and their connection to all living things above, on, and below the land. The Maidu of California's Sierra Nevada are represented in

10 "Lesson in Fire," a poem teeming with dreamlike images that **recalls** the lore of making fire.

recalls:

Song
Makah

Mine is a proud village, such as it is,
We are at our best when dancing.

Twelfth Song of Thunder
Navajo Tradition

The voice that **beautifies** the land!
The voice above,
The voice of thunder
Within the dark cloud
5 Again and again it sounds,
The voice that beautifies the land.

beautifies:

The voice that beautifies the land!
The voice below,
The voice of the grasshopper
10 Among the plants
Again and again it sounds,
The voice that beautifies the land.

②Reread Reread "Twelfth Song of Thunder." What does the poem tell you about how the Navajo view nature?

_____

_____

_____

_____

③ Read As you read, collect and cite text evidence.

- Circle the knowledge or skill that the speaker's father passed on to the speaker.
- Underline the images that can be seen or imagined in the flames.

tend:

Lesson in Fire
by Linda Noel

My father built a good fire
He taught me to **tend** the fire
How to make it stand
So it could breathe
5   And how the flames create
Coals that turn into faces
Or eyes
Of fish swimming
Out of flames
10 Into gray
Rivers of ash
And how the eyes
And faces look out
At us
15 Burn up for us
To heat the air
That we breathe

44

And so into us

We swallow

20   All the shapes

Created in a well-tended fire

4 Reread and Discuss Reread "Lesson in Fire." Discuss what the poet might mean in the final three lines.

SHORT RESPONSE

Cite Text Evidence Reread all three poems. What is the central message of each poem? Cite details from the poems in your response.

_____

_____

_____

_____

_____

_____

UNIT 3
Exploring the Limits

Background Fire is a powerful force, providing light, energy, and heat. Unfortunately, it can also take lives and destroy property. As we learn more about the role of wildfires in the natural world, we are learning to take advantage of their benefits while also protecting people from their destructive power.

Setting a Purpose Read the text to learn about wildfires and the arguments for and against setting controlled fires.

Fire: Friend or Enemy?

Informational Text by Gerardo Benavides

CLOSE READ
Notes

① Read As you read, collect and cite text evidence.

- Draw a check mark next to the definition of a wildfire.
- Circle the event that caused people to start fighting wildfires.
- Underline what happened as a result.

A wildfire is a rapidly spreading fire that burns uncontrollably in the wilderness. In the past few years, many wildfires have burned in wild areas across the United States. Some are caused by
5 lightning strikes, but most are caused by careless people.

For thousands of years, natural fires regularly burned huge areas of wild land. After a series of deadly fires in 1910, land managers would either

10 prevent or quickly put out these fires. As a result, dry, dead plants piled up. During times of high fire risk, such as drought, wildfires could be started by something as simple as a spark from a piece of machinery. The dry, dead plants provided fuel for these fires, making the fire quickly burn

15 out of control. Winds could hurl burning-hot **embers** miles away, **igniting** more fires.

embers:

igniting:

The fire triangle shows the three ingredients of fire.
Remove any of these ingredients, and a fire will die.

②Reread Reread lines 7–16. What is one reason that avoiding wildfires might be a bad idea? Cite details from the text in your answer.

_____

_____

_____

_____

_____

3 Read As you read, collect and cite text evidence.

- Underline text that describes what fire experts do to control fire.
- Circle the benefits of fires in wild areas.

Now scientists are helping land managers harness the power of fire. Just as medical doctors prescribe medicine, these "fire doctors" prescribe fire. They set prescribed
20 fires to improve the health of wild lands.

In states that have had several wildfires, such as Florida and California, fire experts are working in national parks and other wild areas. They set fires to burn dry, dead plants on the forest floor.

nutrients:

25 Ashes from these fires add **nutrients** to the soil. As a result, trees become healthier and plants grow back stronger than before. For some plants, fire is necessary for survival.

When natural fires are stopped, forests become less
30 diverse. In California, some pine and cypress trees cannot spread their seeds without fire. Their seed cones open only if they are heated.

To promote different types of plant growth, fire experts burn away dead plants on the forest floor. The
35 heated cones open up, allowing the seeds to drop onto bare soil where they can sprout.

Experts also use prescribed fires to help birds, animals, and other wildlife. In Florida, some species of birds, such as the Florida scrub jay, rely upon fire to

habitat:

40 maintain the conditions of their **habitat.** Prescribed fire helps the scrub jay and other species survive.

50

Herds of elk live in the Mendocino National Forest near Willows, California. Elk eat many different plants. A burn might be prescribed to encourage the growth of grasses,
45 plants, and freshly-sprouted brush that elk like to eat. As a result, the elk find plenty to eat and their population grows.

Fires are always dangerous, even if they are set by experts to help the environment. A few prescribed fires have spread out of control, but thousands more have been safely
50 contained. Wildfires are by far the most dangerous kind of fire. Many huge wildfires often burn across an entire state at the same time. Land managers can help prevent these dangerous wildfires by planning fires to burn dead plants.

Firefighters continue to bravely fight wildfires. Fire
55 doctors continue to turn this wild enemy into a powerful friend.

④ Reread and Discuss Look at the diagram on page 49. Discuss everyday examples of how you could put out a fire using the information in the diagram.

SHORT RESPONSE

Cite Text Evidence Does the author argue against or in favor of using prescribed fires? What are some specific facts and examples he uses to support his claim?

_____

_____

_____

_____

_____

_____

Background Hot air balloons might not be the fastest form of transportation, but for thousands of people, they are a fun, relaxing way to see the countryside. In this text, you'll read about the invention of the first hot air balloons. You'll also learn what makes them rise and how pilots are able to steer them.

Setting a Purpose Read the text to discover how hot air balloons work.

Riding on Air

Informational Text

CLOSE READ
Notes

① Read As you read, collect and cite text evidence.
- Circle text that tells what causes balloons to rise.
- Underline text that explains what led the Montgolfier brothers to invent hot air balloons.

Every year in early October, the sky above Albuquerque, New Mexico, fills with multicolored hot air balloons. The balloons rise by propane-heated air. They are guided—and

5 sometimes jostled—by undulating wind currents. The International Balloon Fiesta is the largest gathering of hot air balloons in the world. In a way, it is also one of the world's biggest science experiments, demonstrating **buoyancy,**

10 convection (moving heat), and wind power.

buoyancy:

The annual Albuquerque International Balloon Fiesta began in 1972 with thirteen balloons launched from a shopping mall parking lot. Today thousands of visitors attend, relishing the sight of hundreds of balloons in the air.

The Rise of Ballooning

Ballooning began in France in 1783. The Montgolfier brothers, paper-makers, had noticed that paper bags rise when they are held over a fire. They experimented and that summer they launched a balloon made of linen and paper.

15 It carried a rooster, a duck, and a sheep. Two months later, two human passengers went up in a Montgolfier balloon. If their nerves were frayed, who can blame them? Today we consider them ballooning **pioneers.**

pioneers:

②Reread Reread lines 11–19. Summarize the events that led to the first people taking off in a hot air balloon.

_____

_____

_____

_____

_____

53

③ Read As you read, collect and cite text evidence.

- Underline text that explains how a hot air balloon rises.
- Circle text that explains how a pilot guides a balloon.

Hot Air

How do hot air balloons go up? They rely on the same

20 principle that the Montgolfiers used in 1783: convection,
or heat in motion—in this case, hot air filling up a giant
bag. Today the bag, or envelope, is made of supple nylon.
Beneath it is a basket, the gondola, where the pilot and
passengers ride. A frame on the gondola holds one or

25 two burners, which heat liquid propane, turning it to
gas. The gas **ignites** and the air heats up and rises,
pulling the lines holding the balloon taut until it is ready
to take off.

The Ups and Downs of Navigation

From a distance a hot air balloon might appear as frail

30 as a toy. Clouds seem to engulf it as it climbs. What if the
pilot should falter and send the balloon careening in the
wrong direction? In fact, a balloon's pilot is controlling
forces as much as being controlled by them. After going
up, the pilot opens a **valve** at the top of the balloon,

35 letting hot air escape, in order to go down. Meanwhile,
wind currents are traveling crosswise in different
directions at different **altitudes.** The pilot can go up or
down to choose the right wind current and travel in the
right direction.

ignites:

valve:

altitudes:

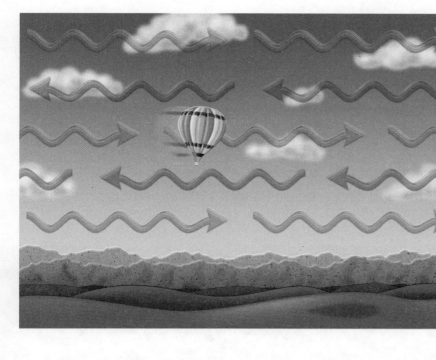

To travel horizontally, the pilot of a hot air balloon uses the burner or valve to climb or drop to different altitudes. Air currents at those levels push the balloon in the desired direction.

④ Reread and Discuss Reread lines 19–39. Discuss what causes hot air balloons to rise. What conclusion can you draw from this about warm air? Cite text evidence in your discussion.

SHORT RESPONSE

Cite Text Evidence How does the diagram on this page support ideas in the text? Cite details from the text in your response.

_____

_____

_____

_____

_____

Background A memoir is a form of writing in which the author shares his or her personal observations of an important event or person. In this memoir, Matthew Henson describes experiences he had while crossing the ice to reach the North Pole with Commander Robert Peary.

Setting a Purpose Read the text to discover what Henson experienced, felt, thought, and observed on Peary's 1909 expedition.

The Pole!

Memoir by Matthew Henson

CLOSE READ
Notes

① Read As you read, collect and cite text evidence.

- Circle the sentences that establish when and where the events of the memoir take place.
- Underline words and phrases that describe Henson's feelings and reactions to events.

In the spring of 1909, Commander Robert Peary's long-held dream was about to come true. The North Pole was only 130 frozen miles away. Captain Bartlett and his team had returned from
5 *breaking the trail and leaving supplies. As the captain headed south and home, Commander Peary, Matthew Henson, and four native Inuit would undertake the final assault on the North Pole. Three years after returning from the Arctic,*

10   *Matthew Henson wrote a memoir about his adventures and*
described their fearful and exhilarating journey to the top of
the world.

It was during the march of the 3rd of April that I
endured an instant of hideous horror. We were crossing a
15   land of moving ice. Commander Peary was in the lead
setting the pace, and a half hour later the four Esquimos
and myself followed in single file. They had all gone before,
and I was standing and pushing at the **upstanders** of my   **upstanders:**
sledge, when the block of ice I was using as a support
20   slipped from underneath my feet. Before I knew it, the
sledge was out of my grasp, and I was floundering in the
water of the **lead.** I did the best I could. I tore my hood from   **sledge:**
off my head and struggled frantically. My hands were
gloved and I could not take hold of the ice, but before I
25   could give the "Grand Hailing Sign of Distress,"* faithful   **lead:**
old Ootah had grabbed me by the nape of the neck, the
same as he would have grabbed a dog. With one hand he
pulled me out of the water and with the other hurried the
team across.

---

*   **Grand Hailing Sign of Distress:** a distress gesture made with both
    arms

---

②Reread   Reread lines 13–29. In your own words, describe the event that
causes Henson to experience "an instant of hideous horror" in "a land of moving ice."

_____

_____

_____

_____

_____

③ **Read** As you read, collect and cite text evidence.

- Underline text that reveals Henson's thoughts and feelings about events.
- Circle important items that were on the sledge Ootah saved.

safeguarded:

30   [Ootah] had saved my life, but I did not tell him so, for such occurrences are taken as part of the day's work. The sledge he **safeguarded** was of much more importance, for it held, as part of its

35 load, the Commander's **sextant,** the mercury, and the coils of piano-wire

sextant:

40 that were the essential portion of the scientific part of the expedition.

    My *kamiks*

Matthew Alexander Henson

45 (boots of sealskin) were stripped off, and the congealed water was beaten out of my bearskin trousers, and with a dry pair of kamiks, we hurried to overtake the column. When we caught up, we found the Esquimos gathered around the Commander,

relieve:

50 doing the best to **relieve** him of his discomfort, for he had fallen into the water also. While he was not complaining, I was sure that his bath had not been any

voluntary:

more **voluntary** than mine had been.

When we halted on April 6, 1909, and started to build
55 the **igloos,** the dogs and sledges having been secured, I
noticed Commander Peary at work unloading his sledge
and unpacking several bundles of equipment. He pulled
out from his *kooletah* (thick, fur outer-garment) a small
folded package and unfolded it. I recognized his old silk
60 flag, and I realized that this was to be a camp of
importance. Our different camps had been known as
Camp Number One, Number Two, etc., but after the
turning back of Captain Bartlett, the camps had been
given names such as Camp Nansen, Camp Cagni, etc. I
65 asked what the name of this camp was to be—"Camp
Peary"? "This, Henson, is to be Camp Morris K. Jesup,*
the last and most northerly camp on the earth." He
fastened the flag to a staff and planted it firmly on top of
his igloo.

---

* **Camp Nansen, Camp Cagni, Camp Morris K. Jesup:**
Fridtjof Nansen, a Dane, and Umberto Cagni, an Italian,
were renowned Arctic explorers. Morris K. Jesup financed
Peary's expedition.

igloos:

4 Reread Reread lines 54–69. What is special about the camp made on April 6?
What can you infer that Peary expects to happen the next day? Cite evidence from
the text in your answer.

_____

_____

_____

_____

_____

_____

⑤ Read As you read, collect and cite text evidence.

- Underline text that shows how Henson feels about Peary's American flag.
- Circle words and phrases that reveal Henson's opinion of Peary.

70 For a few minutes [the flag] hung limp and lifeless in the dead calm of the haze. Then a slight breeze, increasing in strength, caused the folds to straighten out, and soon it was rippling out in sparkling color.

75 The stars and stripes were "nailed to the Pole." A thrill of patriotism ran through me, and

80 I raised my voice to cheer the starry emblem of my native land.

The Esquimos

85 gathered around and, taking the time from Commander Peary, three hearty cheers

90 rang out on the **still,** frosty air, our dumb dogs looking on in puzzled surprise. As prospects for getting a sight of the sun were not good, we turned in and slept,

95 leaving the flag proudly floating above us.

still:

Commander Robert Peary in 1909

This was a thin silk flag that Commander Peary had carried on all of his Arctic journeys, and he had always flown it at his last camps. It was as glorious and as inspiring a banner as any battle-scarred, blood-stained standard of
100 the world. This badge of honor and courage was also blood-stained and battle-scarred, for at several places there were blank squares marking the spots where pieces had been cut out at each of the "Farthests" of its brave bearer, and left with the records in the cairns,* as **mute** but **eloquent**
105 witnesses of his achievements. At the North Pole, a diagonal strip running from the upper left to the lower right corner was cut, and this precious strip, together with a brief record, was placed in an empty tin, sealed up and buried in the ice, as a record for all time.

mute:

eloquent:

* **cairns:** mounds of stones built as landmarks or memorials

(6) Reread and Discuss Reread lines 96–109. Discuss what Henson means when he says that Peary's flag is "blood-stained and battle-scarred." Why has Peary cut pieces out of the flag? Support your ideas with details from the text.

SHORT RESPONSE

Cite Text Evidence What is Matthew Henson's attitude toward Commander Peary? Use evidence from the memoir to support your response.

_____

_____

_____

_____

_____

_____

Background When people take an interest in a community, life goes better for those who live there. This is especially true for communities where earning enough money to live on can be a challenge. Many people who have had success in their lives want to give back by helping out in local communities. This newspaper article describes one such program.

Setting a Purpose Read the text to learn how some pro athletes are helping young people.

The Ball Is in Their Court

Literary Nonfiction by Jeff Morse

CLOSE READ
Notes

① Read As you read, collect and cite text evidence.

- Circle the name of the organization the NBA founded.
- Underline text that describes what the organization is doing and why.

resources:

What would you do if you became rich and famous? Would you choose to keep your wealth to yourself, or would you use your **resources** to help others?

5   Many players from the National Basketball Association
(NBA) have chosen the second path. They give time and
money to community **outreach** programs like *Es Tu Cancha*
(It's Your Court) that help young people. A skeptical
observer might wonder if athletes just want to polish their
10   image. In fact, most have found that doing good means
feeling good. Their motive is to give back to the
communities they play for.

   The NBA founded *Es Tu Cancha* in 2004. The program's
aim is to build or **renovate** basketball courts in Latino
15   communities across the country.

   How do basketball courts help kids? If you're a young
hoops fanatic, it helps to have a place to emulate your
favorite stars. But playing sports is also a great way for kids
to get in shape. Los Angeles Lakers player Andrew Bynum
20   says that *Es Tu Cancha* is "an **initiative** we hope will
encourage kids to get up and get moving in a local
environment that is both safe and fun."

outreach:

renovate:

initiative:

---

②Reread Reread lines 1–22. According to the article, what benefits do
basketball courts offer in local communities?

_____

_____

_____

_____

_____

3 **Read** As you read, collect and cite text evidence.

- Circle text that tells how many courts *Es Tu Cancha* has opened.
- Underline what athletes are saying about the opportunity to help out.

clinic:

So far, *Es Tu Cancha* has opened more than a dozen courts in cities across the nation. On September 26, 2006, the Lakers helped open a new court in the Nueva Maravilla Housing Development in Los Angeles.

Perhaps the best part of the event was when Bynum and coach Craig Hodges hosted a passing and shooting **clinic** for local kids.

donors:

To say that the kids are excited at these court-opening ceremonies is an understatement. But athletes also say that being part of *Es Tu Cancha* helps to keep their lives from becoming bland. Rather than be anonymous **donors,** many stars are proud to show up at the neighborhood courts. "It is an honor for us to contribute to such a great cause," says former Women's NBA (WNBA) player Sheila Lambert.

Former New York Knicks guard John Starks agrees. "It's a great feeling to be a part of something that's so positive," he says.

The Lakers hold court at the Nueva
Maravilla Housing Development.

④ Reread and Discuss Look at the photos in the article. How do you think the boys feel? Discuss how you would feel if your favorite sports star or other celebrity came to your community and shared his or her talents with you.

SHORT RESPONSE

Cite Text Evidence Reread lines 1–40. According to the article, why does the NBA run this program? What other reasons can you think of for why they might run it?

_____

_____

_____

_____

_____

Background The moon has been a familiar sight in the night sky throughout human history, but until the twentieth century, there was no way to visit it or even to learn much about it. In the centuries before space exploration, people asked themselves many questions about the moon and wrote stories to explain its mysteries.

Setting a Purpose Read the play to learn how a Chinese folktale explains why the moon looks the way it does.

The Woman in the Moon

Play, based on a folktale retold by Cynthia Benjamin

CLOSE READ
Notes

① Read As you read, collect and cite text evidence.

- Circle stage directions that tell how the characters act.
- Underline text that tells what problem the emperor and his people are facing.

Cast of Characters

Narrator • Emperor • Hou Yi • Chang E • Hare

SCENE 1

Narrator: The moon is a popular subject in folktales. In China, the tale of Chang E is a central part of the Moon Festival, or Mid-Autumn Festival, which takes place on the fifteenth day of the eighth
5   lunar month. Here is one **version** of the tale.

version:

According to legend, long ago ten suns circled Earth, threatening to destroy all living things with their perilous heat. A frightened emperor called Hou Yi to the palace.

Emperor: *(fanning himself)* Ooh, it is hot! These ten suns
10 are hovering in the sky, cooking us alive. Hou Yi, you are a famous **archer.** Help us!

Hou Yi: I could try to shoot the suns down, Emperor.

Emperor: *(clapping his hands together)* Then do it and save us from impending doom!

15 **Hou Yi:** *(pointing to one of the suns)* May I leave one sun so we can still see what we're doing?

Emperor: Yes, good point.

(Hou Yi points his bow and arrow to the sky and shoots down all but one of the suns. The Emperor smiles and hands Hou
20 *Yi a bottle.)*

Emperor: This **potion** will grant **eternal** life, but be careful. This bottle contains enough for two. Do not drink more than half.

archer:

potion:

eternal:

②Reread Reread lines 1–23. Summarize the problem the characters have solved in Scene 1. What new problem do you predict might occur in Scene 2?

_____

_____

_____

_____

_____

_____

3 Read As you read, collect and cite text evidence.

- Circle what Chang E does when Hou Yi returns home.
- Underline what happens as a result.
- Draw a check mark next to the line of dialogue that explains the purpose for this folktale.

SCENE 2

Narrator: Hou Yi rushed home and began to tell his
25   wife, Chang E, about their good fortune. But before he
could finish explaining, Chang E grabbed the bottle and
drank it all.

Chang E: *(alarmed)* What's happening? Hou Yi, help
me!

30   **Hou Yi:** You weren't supposed to drink the entire bottle!

Narrator: Chang E flew out the door and began an
ascent to the heavens, never to return. Her journey took
her to the moon, where her only companion was a **hare.**

hare:

Hare: I wasn't expecting company.

35 **Chang E:** I wasn't expecting to end up on the moon.

Hare: *(laughing softly)* Ah, the unpredictability of life!

Narrator: Back on Earth, Hou Yi gazed up at the full moon.

Hou Yi: What are those shadowy shapes on the lunar

40 surface? One of them looks like Chang E, and the other looks a lot like a hare!

Narrator: For generations, the tale of Chang E has explained why there is only one sun and why people see shapes on the lunar surface.

45 **Emperor:** Presumably, they are not just random patterns.

Narrator: Meanwhile, it is said that once a year, on the fifteenth day of the eighth lunar month, Hou Yi is able to fly to the moon and visit his wife.

Hou Yi: I'm coming, Chang E!

④ Reread and Discuss Most scenes have just one location or setting, but Scene 2 has two. Reread lines 24–49. Discuss how you might stage the scene to show both settings.

SHORT RESPONSE

Cite Text Evidence Reread lines 24–35. The folktale explains the sun and the shapes on the moon, but it also contains a lesson. What lesson can readers infer from it? Cite details from the play in your response.

_____

_____

_____

_____

_____

_____

© Houghton Mifflin Harcourt Publishing Company

Background Mary Austin (1868–1934) moved west to California with her family when she was young. She loved the desert and developed a deep appreciation for the Native Americans who lived there.

Setting a Purpose Read the poem to discover what inspires the speaker's self-confidence.

A Song of Greatness

Poetry by Mary Austin

CLOSE READ
Notes

① **Read** As you read, collect and cite text evidence.

- Underline what the speaker thinks of when she hears the old men.
- Circle what the speaker realizes when she hears the people.

In "A Song of Greatness," the speaker honors the great deeds of her ancestors. Stories about people who lived long ago can sometimes seem remote, but this speaker feels a deep connection. As you
5   read the poem, think about the kinds of great deeds people perform in today's world.

A Song of Greatness (Chippewa Traditional)
by Mary Austin

When I hear the old men
Telling of heroes,
Telling of great deeds
Of ancient days,
5   When I hear that telling
Then I think within me
I too am one of these.

When I hear the people
Praising great ones,
10 Then I know that I too
Shall be **esteemed**,
I too when my time comes
Shall do mightily.

esteemed:

②**Reread and Discuss** Reread the poem. How old do you think the speaker is? Cite evidence from the poem in your discussion.

SHORT RESPONSE

Cite Text Evidence What influence does learning about the history of her people have on the speaker? Cite text evidence in your response.

_____

_____

_____

_____

_____

_____

Background Did you know that Chinese civilization is 7,000 years old? To appreciate what a long time that is, consider this: the United States of America is less than 300 years old. This text explores some of the artistic and cultural achievements of China's long history.

Setting a Purpose Read to learn about cultural developments that took place during each of China's major dynasties.

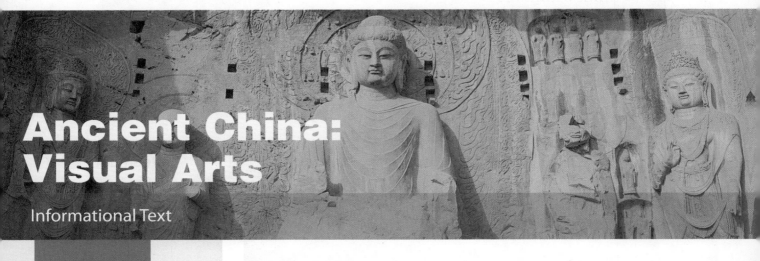

Ancient China: Visual Arts

Informational Text

CLOSE READ
Notes

① Read As you read, collect and cite text evidence.

- Underline each kind of art mentioned in the text.
- Circle the definition of *calligraphy*.

   Chinese civilization began about seven thousand years ago near a river, the Huang He. Over time, ruling families known as dynasties came to power. People skilled in calligraphy,
5 pottery, carving, and metalworking created works of art. Archaeologists today continue to excavate burial sites and buildings. They are finding treasures that give us many details about ancient Chinese culture.

Shang Dynasty: 1650–1050 B.C.E.

10 Calligraphy, or the art of writing, developed during China's first **recorded** dynasty, the Shang. Chinese pictographs were **engraved** into bones or written on bamboo. Other artists from this time formed glazed pottery and
15 bronze figures.

recorded:

engraved:

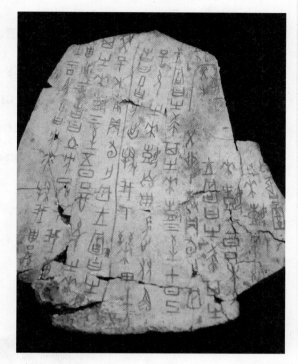

Shang leaders read cracks in oracle bones as answers to important questions. Spoken answers would precede the written ones. Then calligraphers would engrave the answers on the bones.

2 Reread Reread lines 10–15. How is calligraphy related to the fact that the Shang was the "first recorded dynasty" in Chinese history? How was calligraphy used during that period?

_____

_____

_____

_____

_____

3 Read As you read, collect and cite text evidence.

- Underline each word or phrase that describes a kind of Chinese art.
- Circle text that explains how porcelain was made.

jade:

Han Dynasty: 202 B.C.E.–220 C.E.

Artists of the Han Dynasty created elaborate items from bronze and **jade.** Chinese crafts and silk fabrics traveled west on the trade route known as the Silk Road. Western ideas began to enter Chinese thought and art at this
20　time.

The artist who created this bronze figure may have been inspired by mythical flying horses.

Tang Dynasty: 618–906 C.E.

During the Tang dynasty, the art of making porcelain was perfected. A white clay called kaolin was baked at high temperatures, creating a lustrous material like glass.

25 Buddhism became China's **official** religion at this time. Artwork reflected Buddhist ideas, and artists painted the life of the Buddha in colorful natural settings.

official:

This glazed porcelain Tang vase comes from Henan province.

④ Reread Reread lines 16–27. When did Buddhism become China's official religion, and where can you see its influence? Cite evidence from the text in your answer.

_____

_____

_____

_____

_____

⑤ Read As you read, collect and cite text evidence.

- Underline the ideas of Confucius and how these were portrayed by artists.
- Circle what the religion called Daoism emphasized and how its ideas were portrayed by artists.

Song Dynasty: 960–1279 C.E.

philosopher:

The Song Dynasty emphasized the ideas of the **philosopher** Confucius. He taught that there should be
30 harmony between individuals and society. Artists painted everyday pictures that showed people's temperaments. Landscape paintings reflected the ideas of Daoism, a religion that stressed balance between humans and nature.

The Qingming scroll is ten inches high and almost six yards long.
Details in the scroll show parts of city life during the Song Dynasty.

More than just replicas of nature, *shanshui* (mountain-water) landscapes show nature's distinct beauty.

⑥ Reread and Discuss Study the images on pages 78 and 79. Discuss what impresses you about them and what you can infer about the artists' beliefs or the messages they wanted to convey. Point to details in the images that support your inferences.

SHORT RESPONSE

Cite Text Evidence What are some ways in which the headings, images, and captions in this text helped you read and understand it? Use text evidence in your response.

_____

_____

_____

_____

_____

_____

Background The myth of the Minotaur is one of the best known in Greek mythology. Each year, King Minos demanded that the city of Athens send 14 young men and women to the island of Crete to feed a terrible monster called the Minotaur. Prince Theseus of Athens was determined to end this injustice. These texts imagine how newspaper reporters might have covered the events of the myth.

Setting a Purpose Read the texts to see how the events of the myth can be described in the form of newspaper articles.

The
Ancient News

Newspaper Articles illustrated by Marilee Heyer

CLOSE READ
Notes

(1) Read As you read, collect and cite text evidence.

- Circle the sentence that states the main idea of the article.
- Underline details about the main idea, including who, what, when, where, why, and how.

slain:

The Cretan News

Minotaur Slain

The Minotaur is dead. According to reports, the fearsome half-man, half-bull was surprised in its sleep yesterday by Theseus, son of King Aegeus. After a brief struggle, Theseus was able to use a
5   golden sword to end the Minotaur's life. This

action will likely end the tradition of sending Athenian youth into the beast's **lair.** Cretans will recall that a son of King Minos was killed by an Athenian bull. This **prompted** the king's rage and his demand for revenge on Athens.

lair:

10 After the slaying, Theseus and the young men and women in his company escaped from the king's labyrinth. How they did this remains unclear as the maze was thought to be inescapable. The group set sail back to Athens along with a Cretan **accomplice.** Witnesses say this accomplice 15 was Ariadne, a daughter of King Minos.

prompted:

accomplice:

In a related incident, Talus, the bronze guardian of the harbor entrance, was struck and destroyed by a massive wave. Talus was in the act of trying to stop the Athenian **craft** when the wave struck. The black-sailed craft, with all 20 aboard, was able to navigate around Talus and complete its escape.

craft:

② Reread Reread lines 1–9. Summarize how and why Theseus killed the Minotaur.

_____

_____

_____

_____

_____

③ Read As you read, collect and cite text evidence.

- Draw a check mark next to the main idea of the article.
- Underline details that tell when, where, why, and how.
- Circle words or phrases that suggest the information in the article may not be reliable.

THE ATHENIAN NEWS
King Aegeus Drowns

King Aegeus, the long-reigning ruler of Athens, is dead. The king is reported to have plunged into the sea in **despair** at the sight of a black-sailed

25 craft entering Athens's harbor today. Sources close to the king say Aegeus believed that his beloved son Theseus had been killed

30 while on a **quest** to destroy the Minotaur of Crete. A **distraught** Prince Theseus, the **heir** to the Athenian throne, could not be reached for comment.

despair:

quest:

distraught:

heir:

④ Reread and Discuss Reread both articles. If these were real news reports, would you find all of the information credible? Discuss which facts in the articles are credible and which are not. Support your ideas with text evidence.

SHORT RESPONSE

Cite Text Evidence   How does this article, "King Aegeus Drowns," relate to the first article, "Minotaur Slain"? Cite text evidence in your response.

_____

_____

_____

_____

Background You may have never heard of Kush, but this kingdom along the Nile River was once large and prosperous. In this text, you'll read about the history of Kush and what helped make it rich and powerful.

Setting a Purpose Read the text to learn about the ancient kingdom of Kush.

KUSH

Informational Text

CLOSE READ
Notes

① **Read** As you read, collect and cite text evidence.

- Underline details about the geography and climate of Kush.
- Circle details about the Nile River and its effects on Kush.

Land and Climate

Seven thousand years ago, a great society arose along the middle of the Nile River: the kingdom of Kush, also known as Nubia. Kush's civilization was as advanced as that of its neighbor, Egypt.

CLOSE READ
Notes

5   Hills separated Kush from Egypt and the Red Sea. To the south were the tropical forests of central Africa, but much of Kush had a desert **climate.** However, the yearly flooding of the Nile River provided **fertile** soil for animals and crops. In ancient times, Kush was actually wetter than

10   Egypt is today. Huge herds of cattle grazed along the river.

climate:

fertile:

The Kingdom of Kush

Mediterranean Sea

ASSYRIA

EGYPT

| 0 | 250 | 500 Miles |
| 0 | 250 | 500 Kilometers |

ASIA

Key

Kush civilization
1000 B.C.E.–150 C.E.

◉ Capital

Nile River

Kush

Red Sea

Kerma
First capital,
founded
c. 3000 B.C.E.

Napata
Second capital,
700s B.C.E.

AFRICA

Meroë
Third capital,
founded
c. 590 B.C.E.

Kush and the lands around it are in northeastern Africa.

②Reread Reread lines 1–10. How did Kush's location along the Nile allow it to grow crops and raise animals?

_____

_____

_____

_____

_____

© Houghton Mifflin Harcourt Publishing Company

③ **Read** As you read, collect and cite text evidence.

- Underline text that tells about Kush's various rulers.
- Circle text that tells how Egypt influenced Kush.

Queens and Pharaohs

Kush began as a farming community, but over time, it gained in prosperity. The queens of Kush would emerge as powerful and supportive rulers. They shared the throne, and with the kings, they pondered problems

15 facing the kingdom. A queen was known as a *kandake* (kahn DAH kee), or "strong woman."

The armies of Egypt wanted the gold and copper found in Kush. They conquered the kingdom during the reign of Thutmose (thoot MOH suh) I, around 1500

20 B.C.E. Then, after hundreds of years, Egypt's power began to decline. During the 700s B.C.E., the Kushite king Piankhi (PYAHNG kee) conquered Egypt. He began a line of Kushite pharaohs who used many Egyptian ceremonial **rituals.** Later, forced out of Egypt

25 by the Assyrians, the Kushite kings erected a capital farther south, in Meroë (MEHR oh ee).

rituals:

Trade and Culture

The kingdom of Kush carried on a busy trade in gold, ebony, and ivory. Traders on a mission to Egypt could exchange fabric, jewelry, and metal objects for Egyptian

30 goods, such as glass. Kushites also melted down fragments of iron ore to make tools and weapons. Kush's achievements in art, technology, and trade helped it stay in power for nearly a thousand years.

Kushites borrowed many customs from Egypt. They

35 accepted Egyptian ideas of divine figures, worshiping the god Amun. They also **adapted** what they took to create their own culture. At first, the people of Kush carved Egyptian hieroglyphics into the stone of their buildings. By the **Meroitic** period, they had begun to change the

40 hieroglyphs to create different symbols and a cursive **script** that depicted their language. This script reduced the large number of Egyptian symbols to twenty-three signs—an alphabet.

adapted:

Meroitic:

script:

④ Reread and Discuss Reread lines 27–43. Discuss how Egypt and Kush influenced each other. Cite evidence from the text in your discussion.

SHORT RESPONSE

Cite Text Evidence How do the text and the map on page 85 support the idea that the Nile River was an important part of Kush's success? Cite text evidence in your response.

_____

_____

_____

_____

_____

_____

Background Did you know there are about 1,500 active volcanoes around the world, including several in the United States? In fact, in 1980, one famous eruption in Washington State destroyed homes and burned through forests. In this text, you'll read about three destructive volcanoes. You'll also find out what causes volcanoes and where they are most likely to occur.

Setting a Purpose Read the text to discover where most volcanoes are found and what causes them.

Since VESUVIUS

Informational Text

CLOSE READ
Notes

1 **Read** As you read, collect and cite text evidence.

- Circle text that describes the results of the Mount St. Helens eruption and the Vesuvius eruption.
- Underline text that tells what causes volcanoes.

Since the middle of March of 1980, Mount St. Helens in southern Washington State had been producing steam explosions and tremors. Scientists feared that an eruption was coming—

5 and soon.

On May 18, Mount St. Helens did erupt. The volcano **spewed** ash and **pumice** over a 22,000-square-mile area. People who lived nearby had already moved to outlying areas. They were

spewed:

pumice:

10 not able to salvage their homes, but most escaped with their lives.

The citizens of ancient Pompeii were not as lucky. Vesuvius's ashes buried both luxurious homes and meager dwellings. We have learned from their experience. Scientists 15 today closely study active volcanoes to learn more about why and when they erupt.

Our Fluid Earth

Today we know what the Pompeiians didn't: that Earth's interior is always in motion. The theory of plate **tectonics** tells us that Earth's outermost layer, or crust, is made of 20 huge slabs of rock called *plates*. These plates fit together like puzzle pieces. They are thousands of miles across and about fifty miles thick. They float on a bed of molten rock, or magma. Magma is part of Earth's *mantle,* the layer that surrounds its core.

25 The plates don't fit together exactly. They push against each other and slip past each other. This movement can create volcanoes.

tectonics:

2 Reread Reread lines 17–27. What are tectonic plates, and how do they cause volcanoes? Cite text details in your answer.

_____

_____

_____

_____

③ **Read** As you read, collect and cite text evidence.

- In the margin, summarize what you learn from the diagram and its caption.
- Circle text that tells where volcanoes usually occur.
- Underline a warning sign that a volcano could erupt.

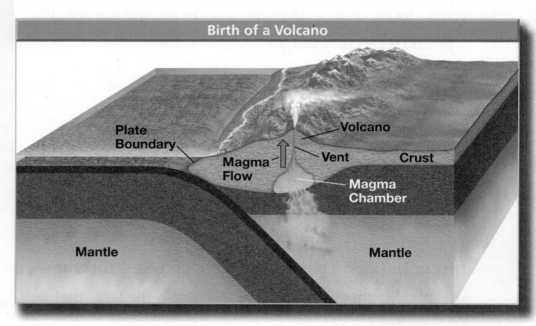

Birth of a Volcano

Plate Boundary

Volcano

Magma Flow

Vent

Crust

Magma Chamber

Mantle

Mantle

When two plates crash into each other, a chain reaction may begin that melts rock in the mantle. The liquid magma can rise through a surface opening called a vent. Lava, rocks, and ash build up around the vent, and a new volcano is born.

Volcano Spotting

No part of Earth is unaffected by plate movement. However, volcanoes usually leave their imprints at or
30   near the edges of tectonic plates. These areas are subjected to more volcanic activity and earthquakes than other areas are. The edges of the plates surrounding the Pacific Ocean are especially active. Scientists call this area the "Ring of Fire."

Lessons Learned

35   Scientists can now recognize some volcano warning signs, such as groups of small earthquakes. Lassen Peak, a volcano in northern California, erupted in 1915, a year after steam blasted through the ground near its **summit**.

summit:

© Houghton Mifflin Harcourt Publishing Company

40 We will probably never be able to predict the exact time of a volcanic eruption. Volcanoes can remain dormant for hundreds of years. Lassen Peak was quiet for 27,000 years before erupting! Still, because we know some of the warning signs, we are much safer than the people who lived in Pompeii's opulent **villas.**

villas:

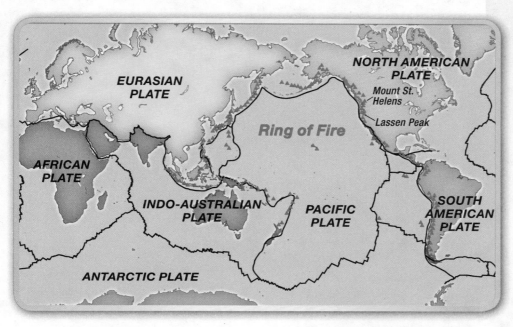

One of the active volcanoes (red triangles) in the Ring of Fire is Lassen Peak. Lassen's boiling mud pots show its volcanic activity.

4 Reread and Discuss Reread lines 28–44 and look at the map. Discuss how knowing about the Ring of Fire can help keep people safe. What can we predict about volcanic activity along the west coast of North and South America?

SHORT RESPONSE

Cite Text Evidence   How does the diagram on page 90 support ideas in the text? Cite details from the text in your response.

_____

_____

_____

_____

_____

_____

UNIT 5
Taking Risks

Background One of the major scientific discoveries of the twentieth century was unlocking the structure of DNA, the building block of living matter. It wasn't just one person's discovery, though. Teams of scientists worked together—and sometimes separately—to figure it out.

Setting a Purpose Read the text to learn about an important scientific discovery and the teams of people who made it.

DNA Detectives

Literary Nonfiction by Dolores Hurley

CLOSE READ
Notes

1 Read As you read, collect and cite text evidence.
- Put a check mark next to what scientists were trying to discover in the 1950s.
- Circle the names of scientists involved in this effort.
- Underline Rosalind Franklin's achievement.

In the 1950s, a race was taking place in England. Two teams of scientists, including one researcher who worked alone, were on their way to making one of the most important discoveries of the

5 century: the structure of the DNA **molecule.** DNA carries the chemical code that determines the characteristics of all living things.

At Cambridge University, James Watson, an American, and Francis Crick, an Englishman,

molecule:

10　were friends and partners. Watson and Crick knew what DNA was, but they didn't know how its parts were connected. They built models of the molecule, using materials scrounged around their lab, but they couldn't make all the pieces fit.

The Twisted Ladder

15　Meanwhile, at King's College in London, Rosalind Franklin was using x-rays to try to photograph a DNA molecule. Unlike Watson and Crick, Franklin did not have a friendly, stable relationship with her **colleague,** Maurice Wilkins. Wilkins had an abrupt manner and often treated Franklin

20　like an assistant.

　　Despite the tension, Franklin continued to work. It took one hundred tries, but eventually, in 1952, she was able to create a clear photograph of DNA. Without her knowledge, however, Wilkins showed the photo to Watson. Some

25　believe that Wilkins did this to be spiteful because of his dislike for Franklin.

colleague:

(2) **Reread** Reread lines 1–26. Based on details in the text, how were the relationships between the scientists on the two teams different?

_____

_____

_____

_____

_____

_____

③ **Read** As you read, collect and cite text evidence.

- Underline text that describes how Franklin's "Photograph 51" affected Watson and Crick's work.
- Circle why Franklin could not receive the Nobel Prize for her work.

Franklin's photo showed a blurry "X." It was a moment of exhilaration for Watson. "The instant I saw the picture my mouth fell open," he said. The photo led

30 Watson and Crick to a new comprehension. It helped them build a twisting, ladder-shaped model of the DNA molecule. On February 28, 1953, Crick walked into a Cambridge restaurant and blurted that he and Watson "had found the secret of life."

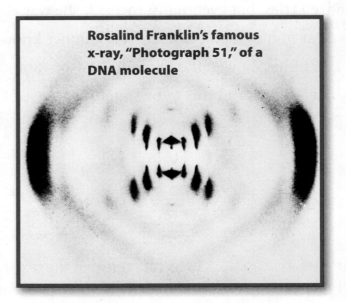

Rosalind Franklin's famous x-ray, "Photograph 51," of a DNA molecule

The Missing Nobelist

35 In 1962 a Nobel Prize in Medicine was awarded to James Watson, Francis Crick, and Maurice Wilkins for their work on DNA. Sadly, the woman whose photo was important to their success was not awarded the prize.

Rosalind Franklin had died of cancer in 1958, and the
40 Nobel Prize is given only to living **recipients.** Some people
think that Franklin's work with
x-rays put her health in jeopardy.
Crick has said that, had she been
alive, Franklin should have received
45 the prize because "she did the key
experimental work."

What Is DNA?

DNA is like an instruction book
for creating living things. DNA
molecules contain four chemicals that
50 attach to each other across the twisted-ladder shape known
as a double **helix.** (See the image on page 94.) The pairs of
chemicals are the "steps" on the "ladder," and the chemicals
can pair up in different patterns. Each pattern is a kind of
oracle, predicting what many of the features of a plant or
55 animal will be.

recipients:

Rosalind Franklin

helix:

4 Reread and Discuss Reread lines 15–34. Was Wilkins's sharing of "Photograph 51" a good thing, a bad thing, or both? What conclusions can you draw about the best way to make scientific breakthroughs? Support your ideas with text evidence.

SHORT RESPONSE

Cite Text Evidence Why did Crick say that he and Watson "had found the secret of life"? Do you agree with his statement? Cite details from the text to support your response.

_____

_____

_____

_____

_____

Background Airplanes and helicopters are common sights in much of the country, and it may seem as though they've been around forever. If you think in terms of human history, though, it hasn't been long at all. And the people flying those aircraft? Most learn to fly as adults, but that is beginning to change.

Setting a Purpose Read the text to learn how one teenager is realizing his goals of learning to fly.

Young Pilot Sets Records

Literary Nonfiction by Linda Cave

CLOSE READ
Notes

① **Read** As you read, collect and cite text evidence.

- Underline text that describes the two aviation records Jonathan Strickland set in 2006.
- Circle details about the people who greeted Strickland on his return.

aviation:

On July 1, 2006, a helicopter pilot named Jonathan Strickland landed his helicopter in Compton, California. Other pilots had done so before him, but this landing was special. It meant
5 a vertical move to the top of an **aviation** record. Strickland's flight to Canada and back made him, at age fourteen, the youngest African American to fly a helicopter on an international roundtrip.

A Record-Breaking Flight

Jonathan's flight had begun nine days earlier, on June 22.

10   Because he was too young to fly alone in the United States, his flight teacher, Robin Petgrave, accompanied him. Flying over **lush** Pacific rainforests and barren fields, Jonathan arrived in British Columbia, where he took tests to fly solo. For many young **aviators,** flying solo is an elusive goal,

15   calling on instinct and practice. Jonathan's dream was to fly solo in an airplane and in a helicopter on the same day. On June 28, he became the youngest person to do so.

On Jonathan's return flight, rough weather conditions arose. The helicopter lurched at times, but it was not

20   decrepit when it landed in Compton. Jonathan's friends and family greeted him, as did members of the Tuskegee Airmen. This African American squadron of the Army Air Corps **endured** the frustration of harsh racism at home while becoming one of the most successful fighter groups of

25   World War II.

lush:

aviators:

endured:

2 Reread Reread lines 1–25. What did the special group of men awaiting Jonathan on his return flight have in common with him? Why might they have been there?

_____

_____

_____

_____

_____

Tomorrow's Aviators

Jonathan Strickland was eleven when he began his flight training at Tomorrow's **Aeronautical** Museum in Compton, California. The museum and its Aviation Explorer Program for teaching young people to fly were 30 **founded** by Robin Petgrave. In return for their lessons, the students perform community service.

Strickland's goals for the future include a lot more flying. He wants to attend the U.S. Air Force Academy, and he hopes to become a test pilot and an airline pilot. 35 "Taking this trip," he said, "gave me the opportunity to see a whole new world and to discover that there is so much more out there for me."

aeronautical:

founded:

In 2008, Jonathan Strickland made solo flights in six different airplanes, including this Cessna 152, in a single day. At age 16, he was the youngest African American male ever to accomplish this feat.

© Houghton Mifflin Harcourt Publishing Company • Image Credits: ©Reed Saxon/AP Images

Tomorrow's Aeronautical Museum Record-Holders

Breean Farfan	Youngest Latina to fly roundtrip across the country	13
Jimmy Haywood	Youngest African American to fly an airplane on an international roundtrip flight	11
Kenny Roy	Youngest African American to fly solo in an airplane	14

④ Reread and Discuss Reread lines 26–31. Discuss why you think the young flyers must do community service in return for their flying lessons.

SHORT RESPONSE

Cite Text Evidence   Does the article support the idea that teaching young people to fly makes sense? Cite details from the chart and the text to support your response.

_____

_____

_____

_____

_____

_____

Background How do you choose which books to read? Do you take the advice of a friend, wait for an assignment from the teacher, or browse library shelves? Some people use book reviews. These are opinion essays in which the writer summarizes the book, states his or her opinion of it, and then supports that opinion with reasons and evidence.

Setting a Purpose Read the book review to learn what one writer thinks of *Number the Stars* and why he holds that opinion.

Book Review:
Number the Stars

Opinion Essay by Carl Wallach

CLOSE READ
Notes

① Read As you read, collect and cite text evidence.

- Circle the writer's claim, or overall opinion of the novel.
- Underline reasons the author gives to support his opinion of the novel.

The award-winning novel *Number the Stars,* by Lois Lowry, is a story about danger, bravery, and friendship. It is set in Copenhagen and Gilleleje, Denmark, in 1943, during World War II. With
5 German Nazi troops occupying Denmark, life is hard for Annemarie Johansen and her family.

Life is even harder for the family of Annemarie's friend Ellen, who is Jewish. The Nazis are planning to move the Jews from

10   Denmark to concentration camps. Feeling contempt for the
German soldiers, Annemarie's family resolves to help
Ellen's family.

      In the course of the novel, Annemarie finds her courage
by confronting her fears. In a tense scene, she is delivering a
15   mysterious package to her Uncle Henrik when she crosses
paths with a group of German soldiers. In harsh voices, they
demand to know where Annemarie is going. They search
through her possessions and interrogate her. After her panic
has subsided, Annemarie responds scornfully. She acts
20   exasperated and begins to cry. Unable to find anything of
interest, the soldiers finally move on.

      Just as memorable as the exciting action are the
characters' relationships. The friendship between
Annemarie and Ellen is the heart of this book. It makes
25   personal an amazing event in history: the heroic actions of
Danish citizens in smuggling some seven thousand Danish
Jews to safety in Sweden.

      Number the Stars is one of Lois Lowry's most powerful
novels. Lowry has tackled a difficult subject with
30   **sensitivity.** Readers who enjoy history as well as action will   **sensitivity:**
appreciate the historical details and the suspenseful plot. All
readers will relate to Annemarie and Ellen's friendship and
the moving examples of the strength of the human spirit.

2 Reread   Reread lines 13–23. What reason for liking the novel does the writer
provide in lines 22–23 that he supports in lines 13–21?

_____

_____

_____

_____

3 Read As you read, collect and cite text evidence.

- Circle the questions the interviewer asks Lowry.
- Underline the main ideas in each of her answers.

An Interview with Lois Lowry

What led you to write about the topic of Denmark during
35 **World War II?**

I think every piece of human history has fascinating
individual stories connected to it. I just happened to
have a Danish friend who told me of her own childhood
in Copenhagen during the Nazi occupation there. With
40 that personal connection, I was able to research the
greater historical **significance** of the events in Denmark.
But I tried to tell them on a personal **scale,** one child's
story.

significance:

scale:

What are the challenges and rewards of writing historical
45 **fiction?**

The challenge is to get it right. There had been some
misinformation about the occupation of Denmark—people
are still telling the (false) story that the king wore a yellow
star in sympathy with the Jews. It didn't happen. I didn't
50 want to be guilty of repeating **myth.** So I read a lot of
history, talked to real people who had been there then, and
tried to write the truth.

    The reward was making an important story available
and interesting to a young audience. There are countless
55 children now who know about the integrity of the Danish
people during that time, and who have been inspired by it.
It's my hope that it has affected the thinking of young
people about issues of prejudice.

myth:

④ Reread and Discuss Discuss Lowry's greatest challenge and reward in
writing *Number the Stars* and how she dealt with her challenge. Then talk about
what you think you would find most challenging or rewarding about writing
historical fiction.

SHORT RESPONSE

Cite Text Evidence   If you hadn't read the novel, would you be convinced to do so
by the book review and the Lowry interview? Use text evidence to support your
response.

_____

_____

_____

_____

_____

Background What represents bravery to you? Maybe it is a person who has achieved status for helping others. Maybe it is an emotion, like the feeling of pride in overcoming a fear. As you read this poem, compare Langston Hughes's ideas about bravery with your own.

Setting a Purpose Read the poem to learn what Langston Hughes means by the title "I, Too."

Home of the Brave

Poetry

CLOSE READ
Notes

① Read As you read, collect and cite text evidence.

- Circle each sentence or group of sentences that makes up a stanza in this poem.
- Underline what the speaker says will happen "tomorrow."

I, Too
by Langston Hughes

I, too, sing America.

I am the darker brother.
They send me to eat in the kitchen
When **company** comes,
5   But I laugh,
And eat well,
And grow strong.

company:

Tomorrow,

I'll sit at the table

10 When company comes.

Nobody'll dare

Say to me,

"Eat in the kitchen,"

Then.

15 Besides,

They'll see how beautiful I am

And be ashamed —

I, too, am America.

② **Reread and Discuss** Reread the poem. Discuss why you think Hughes begins and ends with one-line stanzas that repeat the words "I, too." What is the impact of this repetition? What do the stanzas mean?

SHORT RESPONSE

Cite Text Evidence Is this a poem about where someone sits to eat meals? What larger message can you infer from the lines "Tomorrow, / I'll sit at the table / When company comes"? Use text evidence to support your response.

_____

_____

_____

_____

_____

_____

Background In 2015 a Japanese company released a robot for sale that is able to read and respond to human emotions. Even with a price tag of $1,600, all 1,000 robots sold out in less than a minute. What makes people so eager to interact with robots? This play offers some possible answers to that question.

Setting a Purpose Read the play to discover what Dr. Sneed's secret project is.

Dr. Sneed's Best Friend

Play by Nick James

CLOSE READ
Notes

① Read As you read, collect and cite text evidence.

- Underline details that tell about the setting of this play.
- Circle clues to what Dr. Sneed has been doing all weekend.

Cast of Characters

Dr. Garcia

Dr. Watkins

Dr. Sneed

Sam

SCENE 1

(It is Monday morning at a robotics laboratory. Two scientists enter to find Dr. Sneed, hard at work.)

Dr. Garcia: *(looking around)* Wow, Sneed, it looks as if you've been working all weekend.

5 **Dr. Watkins:** Yes, I thought the data for our new project wasn't due yet.

Dr. Sneed: *(nervously)* Well, actually, ah, I've been working on a **top-secret** project that requires my undivided attention. I didn't even have time to eat breakfast.

top-secret:

10 **Dr. Garcia:** Top-secret? Hmm. Interesting. Care to share any information about it?

Dr. Sneed: Impossible. All I can say is that it's about artificial intelligence.

Dr. Watkins: Well, that's what we all do. Come on, Sneed, 15 you can trust us.

Dr. Sneed: *(pacing)* Fine, if you must know, the project concerns the use of sensors in a domestic setting.

Dr. Garcia: I have an uncanny feeling there is a lot more to it than that—but I've got work to do. Now, good day, 20 gentlemen.

---

② Reread Reread lines 1–20. Make an inference about what Dr. Sneed has been working on all weekend and support it with details from the play.

_____

_____

_____

_____

_____

③ Read As you read, collect and cite text evidence.

- Underline the stage directions that describe the setting and the entry of a new character.
- Circle the stage directions that provide clues to Dr. Sneed's feelings.

SCENE 2

(Later that morning, a small robot knocks and enters, carrying an apple and a glass of milk.)

Dr. Watkins: *(to the robot)* Hello, little dude. Can I help you?

25 **Sam:** *(in a flat, mechanical voice)* No, I do not require any help.

Dr. Sneed: *(rushing over to the robot)* Sam, what are you doing here?

Sam: I am delivering your apple and glass of milk, Dr.

30 Sneed. A healthy snack!

Dr. Sneed: *(in an embarrassed whisper)* Sam, you were programmed to come here at noon. It's only nine o'clock.

Sam: I am sorry, Dr. Sneed. A stimulus in my

motherboard overrode my internal clock.

35 **Dr. Garcia:** What's he talking about?

Sam: You did not eat breakfast, Dr. Sneed. I sensed that your stomach was growling.

Dr. Garcia: Well, Dr. Sneed, I see you've achieved a new interaction between human and machine.

40 **Dr. Watkins:** Yes, I always thought this kind of friendship from a robot was impossible. I suppose this is your top-secret project?

motherboard:

overrode:

110

(Dr. Sneed nods, embarrassed. He takes a big bite of the apple.)

45 **Sam:** Goodbye, Dr. Sneed. *(He turns around and rolls toward the door.)*

Dr. Sneed: Hold on a second, Sam.

Sam: A second is not an object that I can hold, Dr. Sneed.

Dr. Sneed: I didn't mean it literally, Sam. Please go to my

50 office and get two more apples for Dr. Garcia and Dr. Watkins.

Sam: A healthy snack. I will be right back.

(Sam exits, stiffly. Dr. Watkins and Dr. Garcia stare at Dr. Sneed.)

55 **Dr. Garcia:** You spent all weekend programming a robot to bring you food? What a waste of time!

Dr. Sneed: *(shrugging)* That's a matter of opinion. Besides, tomorrow he's making me macaroni and cheese. *(He smiles.)* It's my favorite.

---

④ Reread and Discuss Reread lines 21–59. Discuss how Dr. Sneed feels at the beginning of this scene and at the end. What causes this change? Cite evidence from the text to support your ideas.

SHORT RESPONSE

Cite Text Evidence Do you think Dr. Sneed believes he has wasted his weekend programming his robot? Why, or why not? Cite text evidence in your response.

_____

_____

_____

_____

_____

UNIT 6
Reading Adventures

Background Coping with trash can be a real challenge. Cities and towns must find places to put it where it is safe for people and the environment. But what if that trash happens to be in space? In this text, you'll find out what space trash is, the problems it can cause, and ideas for getting rid of it.

Setting a Purpose Read the text to learn how space trash is made and the dangers it poses.

Space Trash

Informational Text by Mary Carvlin

CLOSE READ
Notes

1 **Read** As you read, collect and cite text evidence.

- Circle the items that make up space trash.
- Underline text that explains why space trash is a problem.

tether:

spectacular:

Oxygen pack. Check. **Tether** cord. Check. Cameras. Check. Thermal gloves. Check. Astronaut Ed White was ready.

5 Boosting himself out of the *Gemini 4* hatch, White began America's first space walk. It was 1965. White beamed as he floated at the end of his twenty-five-foot tether, shooting photographs. Too soon, the **spectacular** walk ended. White made his way slowly back to the spacecraft. But

10 before he handed his gear to his fellow astronaut, he
dropped a spare glove! That glove joined an **assortment** of
odds and ends we call space trash.

assortment:

Over the years, the trash circling around our globe has
grown. Space shuttle *Atlantis* astronauts lost a couple of
15 bolts in space. *Discovery* astronauts lost a spatula while
repairing their shuttle with special putty. A camera, bits of
broken equipment, and even garbage bags tossed out by the
Mir space station have added to the **debris** in space. At least

debris:

10,000 pieces of junk measuring four inches or larger are
20 orbiting our planet. The United States space program tracks
this trash because even though the debris is way up in
space, it could cause us big problems here on Earth if it hits
something.

②Reread Reread lines 9–23. What kinds of things make up the trash that is orbiting Earth, and why is space trash a problem?

_____

_____

_____

_____

_____

It Started with the Satellites

For fifty years now, people have been sending objects into space. Some of those things have been brought safely down to earth, but others have been left in space to drift.

It all began in 1957, when the Soviet Union launched *Sputnik 1,* the world's first artificial satellite. A satellite is anything that revolves around a planet and is held in orbit by the **gravitational** pull of the planet. Our moon, for instance, is a natural satellite. Artificial satellites are objects that people make and send into space.

To launch satellites out of Earth's atmosphere and into space, rockets must travel at least 18,000 miles per hour and fly more than 120 miles into the sky. Such rockets have several powerful engines, a large supply of fuel, and a payload. The payload is the object being sent into the sky, like a satellite. When the rocket fires its engines one after another, the used-up parts of the rocket fall away and become part of space trash.

Sputnik 1 circled Earth every 96 minutes. The United States launched its first satellite, *Explorer 1,* the next year. Scientists used *Explorer 1* to measure how much **radiation** Earth had in its atmosphere. Today, about 850 satellites orbit our planet.

We use satellites every day. When you send a text message or use your cell phone to make a call, a satellite in space sends and receives your messages.

gravitational:

radiation:

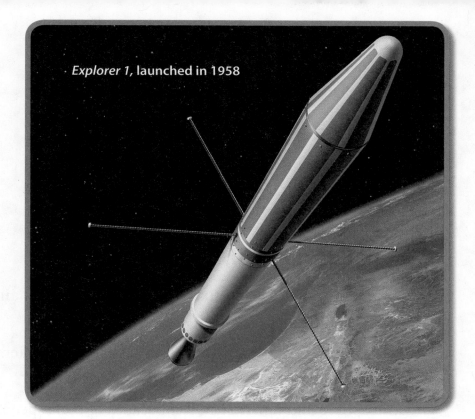

Explorer 1, launched in 1958

50   Satellites also bring television programs from all over the world to people's homes. They send meteorologists (scientists who study the weather) pictures of cloud formations from high above so that the meteorologist on the morning news can tell us whether to bundle up for
55   snow or to grab an umbrella for rain. Some car passengers use satellites about 12,000 miles above us to track where they are on a digital map located on the car dashboard.

When satellites are no longer useful, they become
60   part of the ring of space trash around the Earth. They circle the globe with the pieces of the rocket that first brought them up into space.

④ Reread and Discuss Reread lines 24–62. Why might satellites, in particular, create a large amount of space junk? Cite evidence from the text in your discussion.

In and Out of Orbit

Around our planet lies a sixty-mile-thick blanket of air called our atmosphere. The farther from Earth, the thinner the air becomes. Gravity also becomes weaker. Satellites and space trash orbit outside Earth's atmosphere and remain in orbit because of their speed, or velocity. Earth's gravity holds such objects just enough to keep them from flying off into outer space.

After many, many orbits, a satellite begins to lose velocity. Gravity wins the battle and pulls the object downward. It then drops to Earth at an extremely fast speed. This speed creates **intense** heat that makes the object burn. Spacecraft also heat up when they enter the atmosphere on a trip back to earth.

Russian space experts think *Sputnik I* and the *Sputnik* satellites that followed burned up this way. But the people of Manitowoc, Wisconsin, see things differently. They believe that *Sputnik IV* landed in their town in 1962, right in the middle of Eighth Street. A big chunk of metal lay **embedded** into the middle of the street, while two police officers puzzled over it. Finally, the townspeople sent the 20-pound lump of metal to Washington, D.C. From there, it was returned to the Soviet Union. Today, a brass ring marks the spot on the street in Manitowoc where the chunk landed.

intense:

embedded:

The **incident** in Wisconsin wasn't the only time space trash has fallen into an area where people live. In 1997, a 500-pound rocket fuel tank landed in a field close to a Texas farmhouse. In 2000, people in South Africa found a large, **battered** metal tank in a dusty field. Though it looked like a giant ostrich egg, it was a piece of space trash that had fallen to earth.

Why Worry?

While most objects that reenter Earth's atmosphere burn up, scientists agree that some space trash can survive the fall to Earth. Most of this junk they expect to fall into areas with few or no people, such as the world's **vast** ocean, desert, or tundra areas.

Even though it's extremely unlikely that falling space trash will harm anyone, there's a good reason to worry about space trash. This junk can hit other spacecraft. An object must travel 17,000 miles per hour to stay in orbit. An object the size of a tennis ball traveling at that speed could seriously damage weather satellites, space telescopes, and other instruments used for gathering information.

CLOSE READ Notes

incident:

battered:

vast:

6 Reread Reread lines 94–106. Summarize the dangers that space junk presents.

_____

_____

_____

_____

⑦ **Read** As you read, collect and cite text evidence.

- Circle the sentence that tells why the problem of space trash will continue to grow.
- Underline ideas for getting rid of space trash.
- Circle a word that tells what the author thinks may be the best solution.

In this artist's simulation, a sliver of metal collides with a satellite's solar panel.

Even things as small as chips of paint could damage other objects at such high speeds. A chip of paint made a nick in a window of the space shuttle *Challenger*.

110 Scientists believe the dangers of this whirling junk belt around our planet will continue to grow, as objects continue **colliding** and creating more debris.

colliding:

Clean Up Time!

More than 400 people have traveled in space. Right now, astronauts live on the International Space Station. Scientists
115 are working hard to find ways to keep these astronauts safe from speeding space trash. The National Aeronautics and Space Administration (NASA) even has a special office to deal with the problem.

Scientists have considered ways to get rid of used rockets
120 and payloads in space. One way would be to just shoot used satellites far into outer space. Another way would be to create a special space ship that would travel around snatching and destroying these objects. Still another way would be to zap the trash with powerful lasers.
125 Just as with garbage on Earth, space junk needs to be managed. And in space, as on Earth, it may be that prevention is the best cure.

---

(8) Reread and Discuss Reread lines 113–127. Discuss why prevention might be a better way to deal with space trash than just getting rid of it. How would people prevent space trash?

SHORT RESPONSE

Cite Text Evidence Why might orbiting items as small as bolts, spatulas, and gloves be dangerous for astronauts? Cite details from the text in your response.

_____

_____

_____

_____

_____

Background Sled dogs, also known as Alaskan huskies, are strong runners. With two layers of fur, they can handle the bitter cold temperatures of the Alaskan wilderness. In this text, you'll learn about patrolling Denali National Park using a sled dog team. Though the journal tells a fictional story, it provides many facts about the park and the plants and animals that live there.

Setting a Purpose Read the text to learn about Denali National Park and what it's like to be a park ranger there.

Denali Dog Sled Journal

Realistic Fiction by Terry Miller Shannon

CLOSE READ
Notes

① **Read** As you read, collect and cite text evidence.

- Underline text that describes the rangers' responsibilities.
- Circle details about the climate in Denali National Park.

Saturday, December 8

Today is Saturday, but we Denali National Park rangers have to patrol our part of the park's six million acres every day, so I climbed onto the sled runners and my dog team took off.

5   We have a week-long patrol ahead of us. The dogs looked as excited as I feel when I start on patrol. The dog team patrols started in the 1920s, soon after Denali became Alaska's first park. We

can't take cars or snowmobiles into the park, so the dogs
10 pulling the sleds are our transportation. The dogs allow us
to take care of visitors, haul supplies, and watch to be sure
all is well. We glide over the snow-covered ground. The
ground under the snow is called permafrost. It stays frozen
throughout the year.
15   We were lucky today because there had been no
snowstorm. The trail was clear. We easily traveled the thirty
miles to the first patrol cabin. I was glad to get a fire going
and heat up soup. My traveling companions were tail-
wagging happy to see full dog food bowls!

Sunday, December 9

20 A snowstorm kicked up during the night. All day today I
walked ahead of the team to clear the trail. As I shoveled
snow out of the way, I uncovered a small bush. I marvel at
the plants that manage to survive these **frigid** temperatures.   **frigid:**
    While there are only eight types of trees in Denali
25 National Park, there are many types of shrubs, like alders.
Alders **thrive** in ground that has been disturbed by   **thrive:**
rockslides. Hundreds of other plants survive the winters,
including wildflowers such as fireweed.

---

②Reread   Reread lines 1–28. Summarize what a Denali National Park
ranger does.

_____

_____

_____

_____

_____

③ Read As you read, collect and cite text evidence.

- Underline text that describes the park's wildlife and its geography.
- Circle details that tell what the ranger does when not out patrolling the park.

As I cleared the trail, a wolf howled in the distance,
30 and the dogs howled back.

Thirty-nine types of mammals in the park also
manage to survive the cold. Mice tunnel under the snow
where they can stay warmer. Moose, caribou, and sheep
search for food all winter. Grizzly bears **hibernate**. A
35 long snooze sounds good to me, too!

Monday, December 10

When I radioed in my report to park headquarters, I
learned there was an earthquake early this morning. As
with most of our earthquakes, I never even noticed it.
The quakes are the result of the Denali Fault, which cuts
40 through the park.

The Denali is North America's largest fault. On either
side of this deep crack, the plates of Earth's crust move a
tiny bit all the time. Over millions of years, the plates
shaped the 400-mile **sweep** of mountains called the
45 Alaska Range.

Today in the patrol cabin, I had a chess partner! No, I
haven't taught one of the dogs the game. My partner was
Dr. Chang, a scientist who is studying the park's winter
wildlife. The dogs and I bring him supplies. In return, he
50 feeds us stew and popcorn, and we share his cozy fire.

hibernate:

sweep:

Avalanche from a Denali quake

avalanche:

④ Reread Reread lines 29–50. What would it be like to be a Denali National Park ranger? Cite evidence from the text in your answer.

_____

_____

_____

_____

_____

125

⑤ Read As you read, collect and cite text evidence.

- Circle text that describes the problem the ranger has on December 11.
- Underline text that describes the dangers hikers face.
- Circle details that tell what happened to the Perezes.

Tuesday, December 11

As I left Dr. Chang's cabin today, I received a radio call. Two snowshoers, Andy and Marla Perez, had not checked in at the Wilderness **Access** Center. I passed Wonder Lake, where visitors often go for the view of

55   Denali, which used to be called Mount McKinley after President William McKinley. At 20,320 feet, Denali is North America's tallest mountain. The Native American name *Denali* means "the high one."

People have climbed Denali since 1910. Every year,

60   between May and the first week in July, more than one thousand people try to reach the top of the mountain. About one of every two climbers reaches the top.

There was no sign of the Perezes, so the dogs and I moved on toward the patrol cabin. I saw moose tracks,

65   but no snowshoe tracks. At the cabin, I talked to headquarters. There had been no word from Andy and Marla Perez. Tonight we are all worried about them. Where are they? Are they okay?

Wednesday, December 12

This morning I traveled to Muldrow **Glacier,** searching

70   for the Perezes. I only hoped the Perezes hadn't hiked on a glacier. Glaciers have cracks called crevasses that can be big enough to swallow an entire dog sled. Crevasses are hard to see under snow, so they are very dangerous.

access:

glacier:

Suddenly the dogs yipped and growled. We were face
75 to face with a moose! He didn't look glad to see us—in
fact, he looked angry. I quickly turned the dogs around.
We zoomed off across a frozen river. I could see a small
cabin on the far shore. I headed toward it.

As we approached the cabin, I was surprised to see a
80 kerosene lamp glowing through the window. Even better
were the two sets of snowshoes next to the door. The
Perezes were as excited to see me as I was to see them!
They had gotten lost and weren't able to make their way
back to the Wilderness Access Center. They were lucky
85 to find the cabin.

It was a treat to share our stories. It gets lonely out on
patrol. Andy and Marla gladly agreed to my offer of a
ride in my dog sled for the next two days. They were
tired from all that snowshoeing. As I write this, they're
90 playing with the dogs, who enjoy company as much as I
do.

Muldrow Glacier

6 Reread and Discuss Reread lines 69–91. What does the Perezes' experience
tell you about the risks involved in exploring the park in the winter? What kinds of
things should hikers be prepared for?

127

7 **Read** As you read, collect and cite text evidence.

- Underline a conclusion the ranger draws about how the park used to be.
- Circle details about the south side of the park.

Thursday, December 13

Marla and Andy and I talked about how little Denali National Park has changed over the years. Traveling through it by dog sled feels the way it must have felt in
95   the old days, complete with the dangers and pleasures. Dog sled travel maintains a tradition important to the park.

The Perezes were amazed when I told them the south side of the park is completely different from the north.
panorama:
100   It's a **panorama** of **lofty,** sharp mountain peaks and dark, thick forests. I told them they should fly over it.
lofty:
Flying is the best way to see the area, which is too densely wooded to travel by foot.

Friday, December 14

Marla and Andy are on their way home, but they say
105   they will be back to visit.

I spent the morning doing paperwork. In the afternoon, I gave my report to the ranger who will cover my area next. Before I headed home, I visited the dogs' kennels. I patted each of the dogs I'd just spent a week
110   with, thanking them for taking such good care of me.

I have a few days off now. All the better to rest up for my next adventures on dog sled patrol!

8 Reread Reread lines 92–112. Based on the text, what can you conclude about the north side of the park?

_____

_____

_____

_____

SHORT RESPONSE

Cite Text Evidence Over the years, how might dog sled patrols have helped protect the park's plant and animal life, as well as the surrounding environment? Cite text evidence in your response.

_____

_____

_____

_____

_____

Background Honeybees around the world are disappearing. Why? And what does it mean for people around the world? In this text, you'll read a story about a girl who investigates the disappearance of the honeybees. As you read, you'll find out more about the problems that this disappearance can cause.

Setting a Purpose Read the text to learn how a girl investigates the mystery of disappearing honeybees on a farm.

Vanishing Act

Mystery by Linda Johns

CLOSE READ
Notes

(1) **Read** As you read, collect and cite text evidence.

- Underline text that gives details about the letter the narrator receives.
- Circle text that tells who the narrator thinks sent the letter.

The morning the dead bee arrived in the mail, my mind was already buzzing with ideas. Unfortunately, none of them were about my science project. The letter addressed to me had
5 grabbed my attention.

"A note from my cousin Justin," I thought at first. I nearly tossed the envelope aside, but Justin's handwriting was usually close to impossible to read. This was unusually careful and clear. I opened the envelope and unfolded the

10 piece of blue paper inside. A bee **carcass** fell on my desk.

At least I thought it was a bee. I always have a hard time telling apart flying, stinging insects—such as wasps, hornets, and bees—when they're alive. A dead one was even trickier to identify. The note said:

15 "Thousands more like this one are missing in action. It's a mystery. Call me."

No signature on the note. But it was from Justin. I was sure of it.

I found a magnifying glass and studied the dead bug my

20 cousin had sent. I compared it to images in the encyclopedia. I learned that wasps always have yellow and black stripes, whereas honeybees are often a golden brown. Since bees in cartoons are almost always yellow-and-black striped and cute, you can understand my initial confusion.

25 But the dead insect was definitely a honeybee. I picked up the phone to call Justin.

CLOSE READ
Notes

carcass:

---

2 Reread Reread lines 1–26. What events set this mystery story in motion? Cite details from the text in your answer.

_____

_____

_____

_____

_____

③ Read As you read, collect and cite text evidence.

- Circle text that describes the problem with Grandpa Ray's hives.
- Underline why bees are important to farming.
- In the margin, write your prediction about what Tia will do for her science project.

"Hey, stop sending dead stuff to me," I said when he picked up.

"It got your attention, didn't it?" he replied.

30 "What's going on?" I asked.

"I'm at Grandpa Ray's farm. When we got here on Friday night, he was having a fit because the hives he rented were empty," Justin said.

"Wait a second. Your grandpa rents hives?" I asked.

35 Justin's Grandpa Ray wasn't my grandpa but I'd been to his farm dozens of times. I'd learned a lot about farming from the visits, but I had no idea what Justin was talking about. "Empty hives?"

"Yeah, lots of farmers rent beehives," Justin said,

impatient:

40 clearly **impatient** with me. "Grandpa has beekeepers bring hives here every February for the almond harvest. All the farmers do it. Grandpa said they need millions of

pollinate:

bees to **pollinate** the crops. And that's just for the almond orchards."

45 Raising bees was a much bigger business than I'd imagined. Our class went on a field trip to visit beekeepers when we were in fourth grade. We learned all about pollination from a beekeeper who wore what looked like a white space suit that completely covered

50 her.

I was mostly interested in the beeswax candles and jars of honey that they sold in the gift shop, so I kind of forgot that bees have a bigger job in the scheme of things. If honeybees don't pollinate plants, those plants won't
55 reproduce and make seeds for new plants. Farmers could get **desperate** for bees.

desperate:

"I need you to come out here and take a look. I need you to be my eyes," Justin said.

"What *I* need to do is to come up with an idea for a
60 science project. And it can't be just one of my regular kind of **brilliant** ideas. This has to be *especially* brilliant because the whole town will see it at the science fair. If I don't have something by dinner, Mom will ground me and I'll never get to see you again," I said.

brilliant:

65 "Tia," Justin said with a long, dramatic sigh. "Don't you get it? This *is* your science project. That's why I wrote to you."

"What about my **keen** observational skills?" I asked.
"That too."

keen:

70 Justin was a year ahead of me in school and he knew all about the required sixth-grade independent science project. He was right. An investigation into the missing honeybees *did* sound like a good science project.

---

④ Reread Reread lines 51–73. Summarize why Justin wrote to Tia and wants her to come to Grandpa Ray's farm.

_____

_____

_____

_____

⑤ Read As you read, collect and cite text evidence.

- Underline questions and theories Tia has about the honeybees.
- Circle text that describes Grandpa Ray's questions and theories about the honeybees.

When Mom got back from the store, we decided to
75 take a trip to the farm. I called Justin and arranged to
meet him there in the afternoon.

When we arrived at the farm, Mom went into the
house to visit Grandma Ray. Grandpa Ray took Justin
and me out to the orchards, **narrating** our walk as if we
80 were being filmed for a TV nature program. "Bees
pollinate more than 90 crops in the U.S. We bring them
in every spring for the almonds. We use them for
avocadoes, cherries, and kiwis, too. But look what we
have here." He stopped at a hive, poking it with a stick.
85 "Go ahead and look. Believe me, nothing will hurt you."

I **peered** inside.

"It's empty," I said, taking
a photograph.

"Exactly," Grandpa Ray
90 said.

"Would someone steal
them and then sell them or
rent them to another
farmer?" I asked.

95 "Seems like they'd need to
take the whole hive in order to
make any money," Justin
commented.

Justin was right: There were
no bees at home in this
hive.

"I'm afraid some young yahoo is trying to cause
100 trouble. Probably doesn't realize that without bees there

narrating:

peered:

commented:

won't be as much food," Grandpa Ray said. "So much of what we eat wouldn't be possible without honeybees. In California, the almond crops alone are worth about two billion dollars."

105   "Maybe someone is either **intentionally**—or unintentionally—poisoning honeybees," I suggested.

    I asked Grandpa Ray what kind of fertilizers and pesticides he used on his farm. He assured me his farm used only **organic** fertilizer and that he absolutely would

110 not allow pesticides on food crops.

    "It's possible that someone else might be adding something poisonous, however," I said.

    "If something was killing the honeybees, you'd think I'd have millions of dead bees around here, but I don't.

115 Where did they go? How could they just **vanish**?" Grandpa Ray asked.

    I told Grandpa Ray that I'd like to study the case of the missing bees for my science project. I thought maybe I could answer some of our questions. Grandpa Ray

120 grinned for the first time that afternoon and said, "Tia, I'll give you a quart of honey if you can figure out where they went."

    That made me smile. Justin's grandpa knew how much I loved honey.

intentionally:

organic:

vanish:

---

6 Reread Reread lines 85–124. Describe what Tia does to try to solve the mystery. What questions does she ask?

_____

_____

_____

_____

(7) Read As you read, collect and cite text evidence.

- Circle details about what both Tia and Justin do or contribute to help solve the mystery.
- Underline text that describes what Tia finds out.

125   I started on my project right away and began by taking several dozen photographs around the farm as well as the surrounding landscape.

Was it crazy to think someone would intentionally steal or kill honeybees?

130   When we got back to the farmhouse, I hooked my camera up to Justin's laptop so I could look at the photos I'd taken.

"Tell me what you see there," Justin said, moving his head so he could see from the corner of his eye. Justin's

135   legally blind, but that doesn't mean he's totally blind. He has peripheral vision, which means he can see things off to the side. It takes people a while to get used to how he moves so that he can see their faces. He uses a computer all the time, but it would be next to impossible for him to

140   see any details that would be in the photographs that I just took. I zoomed in on one photo.

"What do you see?" Justin asked, leaning in.

"It's what I don't see," I said. "It looks like a large

transmitter: electricity **transmitter,** but there aren't any wires going

145   into it or coming out of it."

"Sounds like a cell site," Justin said.

"A sell sight?" I asked. "What's that?"

"For cell phones. They pick up cell phone signals."
Justin launched into a long description of how my cell
150 phone worked. My mind was elsewhere.

Could this be a clue?

When we got home, I told Mom I was off to research
the disappearance of the honeybees. In just a couple of
hours of online research I learned that our county wasn't
155 the only one with missing honeybees. Since the fall of
2006, about half of the states reported dramatic **declines**
in the number of honeybees.
Estimates were that some
commercial beekeepers had lost
160 between thirty and ninety percent
of their honeybee colonies. That's a
huge range, but even losing thirty
percent of these hard-working
pollinators could be destructive for
165 farms and, later, for people. Reports
were also coming in from Germany,
Spain, Greece, and other countries
that beekeepers were losing hives.

The buzz about honeybees was
170 that the bees were dying.

declines:

Justin knew it was a cell site in my photo.
Could cell phone signals interfere with
honeybees?

---

(8) Reread Reread lines 125–155. What do Justin and Tia each contribute to the
investigation of the honeybees' disappearance? Cite details from the text.

_____

_____

_____

_____

_____

9 Read As you read, collect and cite text evidence.

- Underline text that describes some possible effects of the disappearance of honeybees.
- Circle what scientists have called the problem and what they think is causing it.

This case sounded more serious all the time. I started thinking about what the disappearance of the bees might mean. I wondered if there would be any more honey for sale. I wondered how people would be affected by a big

175   decrease in the number of fruits and nuts available. It seemed like those foods would definitely get more expensive. It also seemed that I might not get honey for my morning toast even if I figured out what happened to the bees. What if they were just gone forever?

States reporting losses
Non-reporting states

180 I spent the next several months researching why the bees had disappeared. I also decided to title my science project "Vanishing Act: The Mystery of the Disappearing Honeybees." My title was a little more interesting than "Colony Collapse Disorder" (CCD), which is what scientists

185 had officially dubbed the phenomenon. Cell phone towers, certain pesticides, and drought were at first possible **culprits** for CCD. Eventually all were ruled out.

By the time I presented my science project at the end of the school year, the best theory available was that a virus

190 had caused bees to weaken and, eventually, die. Some bees may have left the hive and then became too weak to pollinate or to return.

I scored a 98 percent on my presentation of "Vanishing Act." The score wasn't perfect, but it was pretty good.

195 I really scored on the honey, though. Grandpa Ray dropped off some of the best honey I've ever tasted after he saw my presentation. I don't know where he got it, but that's a mystery I won't worry about solving just yet.

culprits:

⑩ Reread and Discuss Reread lines 171–179. Discuss how the disappearance of the honeybees could affect the world's food supply. What might it mean for countries that rely on foods pollinated by honeybees?

SHORT RESPONSE

Cite Text Evidence What kind of character is Tia? Do her reasons for investigating the mystery change by the end of the story? Cite text evidence in your response.

_____

_____

_____

_____

_____

Background Elephants are the world's largest land animals. With that huge body comes a massive brain. But how smart are they really? In this play, you'll read about three kids who go to Kenya to see elephants up close. They learn about how elephants live and about the special characteristics that set them apart from other animals.

Setting a Purpose Read the text to learn about African elephants.

Elephants on the Savannah

Readers' Theater by Beth Geiger

CLOSE READ
Notes

① **Read** As you read, collect and cite text evidence.

- Underline details about the play's setting.
- Circle text that explains what the characters are planning to do.

Cast of Characters

Narrator

Judith: Kenyan ranger/guide

Jordan

Maya

Antonio

Narrator: In Kenya, East Africa, it's just before dawn in Amboseli National Park. This famous park is a great place to watch African elephants. Maya, Antonio, and Jordan have traveled here from the United States. Now they are
5 ready for their first day on the **savannah.**

Judith: Good morning! How was your first night in Amboseli?

Jordan: I'm still tired!

Judith: Don't worry. You'll have a chance to rest after our
10 morning drive. Does everyone have sunscreen and a water bottle?

Maya: It's hard to remember sunscreen when it's still dark out.

Judith: Ready to see African elephants?

15 **Antonio:** Definitely! I've got my **binoculars.**

Judith: This time of day the elephants are usually heading towards the swamps. So we'll go in that direction too.

Narrator: Jordan, Maya, and Antonio follow Judith to her jeep and climb in. It gets lighter as they go.

20 **Maya:** Wow, there's Mount Kilimanjaro! That is one big mountain.

Antonio: Hey, I see elephants!

savannah:

binoculars:

---

2 Reread Reread lines 1–22. Summarize what has happened in the play so far.

_____

_____

_____

_____

_____

trumpets:

Narrator: Eleven elephants are slowly walking near the road. The herd includes two babies. One elephant

25 **trumpets** loudly.

Jordan: Okay! I'm awake!

Antonio: Wow. That first elephant is one big dude! He must be ten feet tall. And look at those tusks.

Judith: Actually, that "dude" is a female. Herds are

30 family groups led by the oldest female. She is called the matriarch.

Maya: I like that!

Judith: And by the way, African elephants have tusks whether they are male or female.

35 **Jordan:** Do the herds always stay together?

Judith: The females and young elephants do. All the females in a herd help teach and protect the calves. They're like "extra moms."

Antonio: Which ones are the dads?

40 **Judith:** No dads here. Grown-up males are called bulls. They can weigh six tons or more. Bulls leave their herds when they are about fourteen. After that they live mostly alone.

Antonio: The elephants have stopped walking. It seems

45 like they're listening to something.

Jordan: Want to hear a cool thing I read about elephants?

Maya: I'm all ears.

Jordan: Elephants listen through their feet. Right, Judith?

50 **Judith:** Their feet have special **vibration** sensors. Elephants **detect** rumbles through the ground. That way they can communicate with other elephants miles away. Elephants make all sorts of other noises. They can scream, grunt, or trumpet. Each sound means something different.

55 **Maya:** Antonio, what are you looking at?

Antonio: Check it out. There's another family group way down in the valley. Maybe this herd is talking to that one.

Maya: And now these elephants are walking in that direction. Can we go that way too?

60 **Narrator:** The four get in the jeep and head toward the swamp, across open savannah. They park near the elephants.

Maya: Yikes. Aren't we close enough? These are big guys. I mean, big gals.

65 **Judith:** Don't worry. The females are usually pretty gentle. The ones here in Amboseli are used to jeeps. Let's watch for a while.

Jordan: They sure flap their ears a lot.

Maya: I read about that. The ears have lots of blood veins
70 in them. Flapping cools the blood off in hot weather.

Jordan: Now they're wading in the swamp.

④ Reread Reread lines 23–43. Why are elephant herds made up of only females and calves? Cite text evidence in your answer.

_____

_____

_____

_____

⑤ Read As you read, collect and cite text evidence.

- Underline details about how elephants treat the bones of dead elephants.
- Circle text that describes what elephants remember.

Antonio: Looks like bath time. Look at them spray their own backs with their trunks.

Maya: Those elephants are smart. It's getting hot out

75   here!

Judith: Hey gang, it's almost 9:30. Let's head back to camp. We'll have breakfast. Then later, we can cool off in the camp pool.

Jordan: Yes!

80   **Maya:** Sort of like the elephants.

Antonio: Won't we miss some action?

Judith: Not really. During the hottest part of the day, elephants mostly rest in the shade. I want to show you something on the way back.

85 **Narrator:** They drive for a few minutes. Judith parks near a pile of big bones.

Jordan: Wow. Did an elephant die here?

Judith: Yes. About two years ago one of the matriarchs died.

90 **Maya:** Why are all the bones scattered?

Judith: Elephants **mourn** their dead. They still stop by here to gently pick up the bones with their trunks. That's why the bones are spread around.

Antonio: I guess they must remember the matriarch.

95 **Judith:** They seem to. They also remember people. For example, they will sometimes approach familiar humans, such as researchers they've seen before.

Narrator: The group heads back to camp. Soon, all four are in the pool. The African heat is intense. But by late
100 afternoon it begins to cool off. Shadows become longer as evening approaches.

Judith: Okay, it's four o'clock. Everyone ready to continue our safari?

Maya: Let's go! Do you think we'll get to see elephants
105 eating?

Antonio: I've heard they need at least three hundred pounds of food a day.

mourn:

⑥ **Reread** Reread lines 85–107. What can you infer about elephants from the way they respond to the bones of dead elephants?

_____

_____

_____

_____

_____

⑦ Read As you read, collect and cite text evidence.

- Underline details about an elephant's trunk.
- Circle how fast an elephant can run.

Narrator: The four climb back in the jeep. They drive for a few minutes. Then they park in the shade of an
110 acacia tree.

Jordan: There they are. Are those the same elephants we saw before?

Judith: Yes. See the two calves? They are hiding between their mother's legs.

115 **Maya:** Did you see that? That elephant picked up a single blade of grass with her trunk! How could she do that?

Judith: There are at least 40,000 muscles in an elephant's trunk. All those muscles mean they can move
120 their trunks very **precisely.**

Jordan: Those trunks can really **multi-task.**

Judith: They sure can. Elephants use their trunks to express emotion, eat, smell, drink, touch, make noise, and move things.

125 **Antonio:** Check it out. That big elephant is trying to tear out that tree with her trunk. Wow. She did it! She knocked over the whole tree.

Maya: Now she's eating the leaves off the top. So is that calf. How cute.

130 **Jordan:** I hear buzzing. Do elephants buzz, too?

Narrator: Suddenly the matriarch begins to run away. The other elephants follow in a hurry.

precisely:

multi-task:

146

Judith: Oh no! The trunk of that tree contained a bees' nest! See the bees swarming into that one elephant's eyes?

135 **Antonio:** I had no idea elephants could run that fast.

Judith: They can run twenty-four miles per hour. We don't want to get stung either. Let's follow the elephants' lead and get out of here.

Narrator: Everyone piles into the jeep and they zoom away
140 fast.

Maya: Whew. That was close. I'm glad no one was stung.

Jordan: Why is such a big animal afraid of bees?

Antonio: Yeah, isn't their skin too thick to sting through?

Judith: Bees can sting the tender skin behind their ears.
145 Bees can even go up an elephant's trunk.

Jordan: Ouch!

Judith: Let's head back to camp. We'll see more elephants tomorrow. How did you like your first day on the savannah?

Maya: It was fantastic.

150 **Antonio:** It sure was! Thank you, Judith.

Jordan: I can't wait to get up tomorrow morning!

---

8 Reread and Discuss Reread lines 115–151. What do Maya, Antonio, and Jordan think about elephants? Would you feel the same way? Cite text details in your discussion.

SHORT RESPONSE

Cite Text Evidence   What does the author of the play want readers to believe about elephants? Cite details from the text in your response.

_____

_____

_____

_____

_____

Background Every year, dozens of tornadoes sweep across parts of the United States. Hurricanes occur less frequently, but they are just as dangerous. What do we know about individual storms, and how do we know it? In this text, you'll read about the people who risk danger to chase tornadoes and hurricanes.

Setting a Purpose Read the text to learn why people chase tornadoes and hunt hurricanes.

Storm Chasers

Informational Text by Karen Ingebretsen

© Houghton Mifflin Harcourt Publishing Company • Image Credits: ©Creative Travel Projects/Shutterstock; ©The Morning Sun, Andrew D. Brosig/AP Photo

CLOSE READ
Notes

① Read As you read, collect and cite text evidence.

- Underline text that describes what storm chasers do.
- Circle text that tells what storm spotters do.
- Draw a box around the caption that tells where tornadoes form.

Outside, a long siren sounds. On the radio, an announcer says: *"The National Weather Service reports a tornado moving east of Johnstown at 40 mph."*

5   If we heard a warning like this, most of us would do what we're supposed to do. We would head for shelter indoors. We would retreat to the basement, or to an **interior** hallway or room such as a closet, staying away from windows. We

interior:

148

10 would use blankets or pillows to cover our bodies and wait for the storm to pass.

But a small group of scientists and researchers would head in the opposite direction—right toward the storm. These people, known as *storm chasers,* **pursue** tornadoes in

15 specially **equipped** cars, vans, and trucks. They hope to arrive in time for the worst of the weather, so that they can collect as much information about the storm as possible.

Other storm trackers stay closer to home. These trained volunteers, known as *storm spotters,* keep a close watch on

20 the weather in their own community. They pass along storm information to local weather agencies. Sometimes even **sophisticated** radar devices don't pick up storms, and the trained eye of the storm spotters can help to save lives. Listen closely to weather reports on your local TV stations

25 and you may hear the forecasters talk about reports they receive from storm spotters.

Tornadoes can strike at any time of year in the United States, but they are generally most common from late winter through

30 mid-summer.

CLOSE READ
Notes

pursue:

equipped:

sophisticated:

Tornadoes, like this one near Gruver, Texas, usually form in a large area of the U.S. called Tornado Alley, located between the Rocky Mountains and the Appalachian Mountains.

② **Reread and Discuss** Reread lines 12–30. Discuss the difference between storm chasers and storm spotters. Why might storm spotters be important in places like Tornado Alley?

③ Read As you read, collect and cite text evidence.

- Underline text that tells what hurricane hunters do.
- Circle details about the first storm chaser.
- Underline text that describes the history of hurricane hunting.

Hurricane Hunters

Storm chasers don't just follow tornadoes. *Hurricane hunters* take special training to fly planes right into the center of hurricanes and other severe **tropical** storms. Outside, heavy rain and high winds batter the aircraft.

35 Inside, the noise is deafening. Despite the roar and the roller coaster ride, the crew carefully collects information on temperature, air pressure, wind speed, and wind direction. This information will be used to help predict the size, strength, and path of the storm.

40   After flying through the solid ring of thunderstorms that make up the wall of the hurricane, the plane enters a place of near-silence—the eye of the hurricane. Sometimes in this calm center, the hurricane hunters see blue sky, sun, and even stars. But the plane still has to go

45 back through the **menacing** storm before returning home. In fact, most hurricane hunters make at least four trips through the storm before returning to land!

        The hurricane season runs from about June through November in the Pacific and Atlantic oceans.

tropical:

menacing:

Pioneers of Storm Chasing

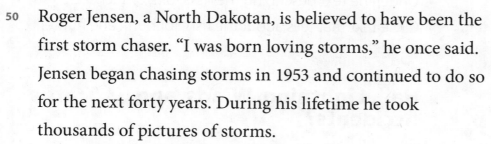

50　Roger Jensen, a North Dakotan, is believed to have been the first storm chaser. "I was born loving storms," he once said. Jensen began chasing storms in 1953 and continued to do so for the next forty years. During his lifetime he took thousands of pictures of storms.

55　　　A scientist named Howard Bluestein had an early introduction to storms. In 1954, when Bluestein was five, a hurricane blew the shingles off the roof of his family's house. When he grew up he decided to make storm study his life's work. Today, Bluestein studies storms as a
60　researcher and professor of **meteorology** at the University of Oklahoma. The movie *Twister* was inspired in part by Bluestein's work.

　　　Hurricane hunting began in World War II, when a U.S. Air Force training aircraft flew into the eye of a hurricane
65　on a dare. To prove his plane's strength, American pilot Colonel Joseph Duckworth told the British that he could fly into the eye of a hurricane. After doing so, Duckworth **pioneered** the science of hurricane hunting.

meteorology:

pioneered:

④ Reread Reread lines 50–68. Summarize what the section "Pioneers of Storm Chasing" is about.

_____

_____

_____

_____

_____

(5) Read As you read, collect and cite text evidence.

- Underline text describing the risks for storm chasers.
- Circle text that tells about the risks for hurricane hunters.

Hail, Lightning, Winds, and . . . Traffic Accidents?

Being in a severe storm is dangerous. Storm chasers can
70 be struck by flying debris or by baseball-sized hail. They
can be trapped by flash floods or downed power lines. Fortunately,
75 most professional storm chasers keep a safe distance from the deadly storm center—
80 usually one to two miles. They respect the power of the storm.

Lightning is also a great risk to storm chasers.
85 Lightning strikes injure **scores** of people each year. The risk rises for storm chasers, who spend more time than the average person in the most extreme weather that Mother Nature serves up.

But the riskiest part of storm chasing is actually
90 driving to the storm. Crashes happen because drivers are hurrying to reach the heart of the storm and are looking at the sky instead of the road ahead of them. Blowing

scores:

© Houghton Mifflin Harcourt Publishing Company • Image Credits: ©Eric Nguyen/Corbis

dust, heavy rain and fog, hail, skidding on wet pavement, running out of gas, and getting stuck in mud can also make

95 the chase difficult and dangerous.

Hurricane hunters face a different set of risks because they are flying an airplane through the most powerful part of a storm. Violent winds can shake the plane severely, making it difficult to fly. Equipment inside the plane can

100 get tossed around, causing possible injury. The wind can also damage the aircraft, and a sudden blast can send a plane **plunging** into the ocean.

Storm spotting and storm chasing should never be done without proper training, experience, and equipment.

105 Hurricane hunting is an activity for experts. For most of us, the best way to experience storm chasing is by watching a TV documentary or movie! As long as there are storm chasers filming the most dramatic weather events, we can sit in the safety of our homes and movie theaters and

110 comfortably experience nature at its wildest.

plunging:

---

6 Reread and Discuss Reread lines 69–102. Discuss what it takes to be a storm chaser or hurricane hunter. What qualities would a person need to have? Cite text evidence to support your ideas.

SHORT RESPONSE

Cite Text Evidence   How do the photographs and headings help readers understand the text? Cite details from the selection in your response.

_____

_____

_____

_____

_____

Acknowledgments

"I, Too" from *The Collected Poems of Langston Hughes* by Langston Hughes, edited by Arnold Rampersad with David Roessel, Associate Editor. Text copyright © 1994 by The Estate of Langston Hughes. Reprinted by permission of Alfred A. Knopf, an imprint of Knopf Doubleday Publishing Group, a division of Random House LLC, and Harold Ober Associates Incorporated. Any third party use of this material, outside of this publication, is prohibited. Interested parties must apply directly to Random House LLC for permission. All rights reserved.

"Lesson in Fire" by Linda Noel from *The Dirt is Red Here: Art and Poetry from Native California,* edited by Margaret Dubin. Text copyright © 2002 by Linda Noel. Reprinted by permission of Linda Noel.

"A Song of Greatness" a Chippewa traditional rhyme from *The Children Sing in the Far West* by Mary Austin. Text copyright © 1956 by Mary Austin. Reprinted by permission of Houghton Mifflin Harcourt Publishing Company.